AF479236

RELIGION
and our
Divided Denominations

RELIGION
and our
Divided Denominations

Edited by
Willard L. Sperry

BY

WILLARD L. SPERRY
JOHN LaFARGE, S.J.
JOHN T. McNEILL
LOUIS FINKELSTEIN
ARCHIBALD MacLEISH

Essay Index Reprint Series

BOOKS FOR LIBRARIES PRESS
FREEPORT, NEW YORK

Originally published as Volume I of
Religion in the Post-War World

Copyright 1945 by the
President and Fellows of Harvard College

Reprinted 1971 by arrangement with
Harvard University Press

INTERNATIONAL STANDARD BOOK NUMBER:
0-8369-2201-8

LIBRARY OF CONGRESS CATALOG CARD NUMBER:
74-128315

PRINTED IN THE UNITED STATES OF AMERICA

CONTENTS

INTRODUCTION

How far can the 256 religious denominations listed in the last census serve the cause of a unified national life? We profess our faith in "one nation, indivisible, with liberty and justice for all." The actual facts of our religious life reveal a widely and badly divided people as far as organized religion is concerned.

The founding fathers of the republic were intent, above all else, on winning freedom for themselves and their fellow-countrymen. The idea of liberty took precedence over all other ideas. That emphasis is reflected in the jealousy which America has always had for religious freedom, whether of individuals or of churches. The Constitution safeguards those liberties, primarily through the formal separation of church and state.

This separation, as we shall see in a later chapter, is a relatively modern solution of the problem involved. Although we take it as a matter of course, we should realize that in separating church from state we have embarked on an adventure for which, prior to the latter part of the eighteenth century, there was little or no precedent in Christendom.

The average American is more jealous for his religious rights, or the rights of his denomination, than concerned with his total duties as a believer. Meanwhile our denominationalism, with its divided and subdivided sects, is a less and less serviceable medium for the expression of the life of a country in which government is increasingly centralized and the apparatus of daily life more and more standardized.

How can we preserve the precious heritage of religious liberty at the same time that we devise ways and means for an expression of the common or corporate spiritual life of our people as a whole? To this problem the contributors to the volume in hand address themselves. A preliminary chapter deals with the chaotic facts. Then follow three chapters in which spokesmen for the major religious traditions of the country—Roman Catholicism, Protestantism, and Judaism—each tell us what the ideal of unity is within his own body, what diversities are compassed by that body, how the corporate life of the entire group finds unified expression and how far it is possible for each to coöperate with the others.

Then follows a chapter on Humanism which is a recognition of the fact that outside formal organized churches there is a great body of persons, mainly, perhaps, in our educational institutions and in the professions or in the arts, who are idealists and loyal servants of their fellow men, but who find themselves intellectually unable to profess the traditional faith in God. An English bishop has said that fifty per cent of the intelligent people of the modern world are humanists. These persons, though ecclesiastically unorganized, deserve recognition.

Contributors to this volume in the series are:

The Reverend Willard L. Sperry, Dean of the Harvard Divinity School and chairman of the Board of Preachers to the University.

The Reverend John LaFarge, S.J., Harvard, A.B., '01, editor of the National Catholic Weekly, *America*, founder and chaplain of the Catholic Interracial Council, director of the Catholic Rural Life Conference, former vice-president of the American Catholic Historical Association.

Professor John T. McNeill, a member of the faculty of the Union Theological Seminary, New York, teaching in the field of Church History; formerly lecturer and professor at Queen's University, Ontario, Knox College, Toronto, and the Divinity School of the University of Chicago.

Dr. Louis Finkelstein, President of the Jewish Theological Seminary of America, New York City, who has served as a member of the executive council, or president, of the Rabbinical Assembly, the United Synagogues of America, and the Hillel Foundation.

The Honorable Archibald MacLeish, Librarian of Congress 1939-1944, appointed Assistant Secretary of State in 1944. His *Conquistador* won the Pulitzer poetry prize in 1932.

Willard L. Sperry
Editor

Harvard University
Cambridge, Massachusetts

*Religion
and our
Divided Denominations*

Willard L. Sperry

·1·

Our Present Disunity

WE AMERICANS have been passing through a time of testing for which there is no precedent in our history. Total war, which has been forced upon us by the enemy, has taxed our resources heavily. In this hour of need the natural wealth of the country has served us well. We have drawn, also, upon the moral and spiritual reserves of our national character. The chief of these reserves is that quality of American life which has been described as our "immense and indomitable optimism." This native habit of hopefulness is, perhaps, our greatest single asset.

Meanwhile, needing common convictions and a common mind to sustain our common purpose, we are made freshly aware of the "varieties of religious experience"—to use the familiar title of a now classical book—which obtain in America. There are, according to the last federal census, 256 religious denominations in the United States. The emergency of battle at the fighting front warrants chaplains in ministering freely not only to members of their own communions in the Army and Navy, but in serving all sorts and conditions of men in a truly catholic spirit. Catholic,

Protestant, and Jew, as we shall be told in a later volume in this series, work together amicably and effectively. So also, on the home front, the many forms of social service asked of civilians cut across all denominational lines and make for a felt sense of moral unity throughout the land.

On the other hand this awareness of spiritual solidarity is not a faithful transcript of the permanent peace-time facts of American culture. By its very novelty it serves as a comment upon the chronic disunity of our religious life. In matters religious we Americans enjoy a freedom which is one of our most treasured rights. But this very freedom has been the occasion and is still the warrant for the multiplicity of our denominations. Can we afford this disunity indefinitely? Or ought we to be attempting to heal our unhappy divisions, as between church and church? Are the lessons learned in an emergency the prophecy of a more consolidated religious life hereafter? These are the sober second thoughts that will persist when the fighting is over.

Religious denominationalism, as we know it in America, is a relatively recent phenomenon. The word itself did not come into general circulation in this connection until the eighteenth century. Over most of the centuries of the history of "Christendom" some one church has been recognized as the acknowledged partner of the state. For twelve hundred years, from the fourth to the sixteenth century, this was in western Europe the undivided Catholic Church. With the breakup of the unified life of the Middle Ages and the advent of modern nationalism in Europe the principle of a union between church and state persisted, but was restated in countless particular instances. The historic Peace of Augsburg, 1555, immediately concerned with religious differences in Germany, proposed the formula *cujus regio, ejus religio*—the religion of any given principality shall be that of its ruling prince. In general this formula was accepted throughout western Europe and resulted in the established state churches of the divided nations. State and church remained the order of the day, and in many lands that partnership still survives, most notably perhaps in Scandinavian lands, but more familiar to most of us in the established Church of England.

No religion, however, has ever been able to persist unmodified century after century. Religious movements tend to bifurcate and proliferate. Therefore every church breeds within its own borders sectarian movements which usually begin as an attempt to reform the church from within, and more often than otherwise, unless suppressed by outright persecution, end in schism. The standard design of formal religious life in Europe over the last four hundred years has been, therefore, that which Troeltsch calls the "church-sect" pattern. There is in any given instance one dominant church, formally acknowledged by the state and united with it. This church has peculiar privileges, both political and economic. It has direct access to government; more often than otherwise it receives much of its support from government. Even when, as in more recent times, its political influence is on the wane and it no longer dips deep into public coffers, it still enjoys great social prestige. At public functions in England the Archbishop of Canterbury follows directly after the Royal Family, taking precedence over the Prime Minister and all other officers of state.

With the sects it is otherwise. For a century after the Reformation they were persecuted and harried from place to place. Holland was their chief asylum. These sects, and they were many in number, were mainly attempts of eager and earnest souls to "complete the work of the Reformation," to purify what were felt to be the imperfectly reformed state churches in their several lands. With the passage, in due time, of belated Acts of Toleration the sects no longer lived in naked peril, but still remained without formal relation to the state and without the rights and privileges of an establishment. We know these bodies in England as "Nonconformists" and "Dissenters." Their ancient grievances have been long since redressed and they no longer suffer legal disabilities, but so long as the Anglican establishment persists as the state "church," they must continue to be classified as "sects."

Our earliest colonists brought to these shores the church and state, and the church-sect patterns of religious life. Some of them came here as refugee sects and proceeded to install themselves as churches, persecuting in turn rival bodies. This was particularly true of New England Congregationalism which was the acknowledged state church in these parts. Quakers, Baptists, Catholics, suffered at their hands. In the southern colonies, beginning with Virginia, the Episcopal Church was the local establishment. There is a long history there of opposition to the advent of Baptists and Presbyterians. The Catholic colony of Maryland succeeded for some time in vindicating the principle of religious toleration, but passed eventually under Anglican jurisdiction in religious affairs. Pennsylvania was the one great haven of refuge for persecuted sectarians coming from Europe. In particular countless small German groups came early and were made welcome. They survive there to this day as witness to Penn's initial generosity and to their own inherent vitality.

The American Revolution was, however, mainly inspired and engineered by the men of New England and Virginia, and in both these quarters the principle of a state church was still recognized and in force. It is true that the English Act of Toleration, promulgated in 1689, following the Revolution of 1688 and the accession of William and Mary, was relayed to the American colonies as binding upon them as well as upon the homeland. But distances were great and the Act was often more honored in neglect than in observance. Sectarians could no longer be martyred, as four Quakers had been on Boston Common, but they were at the best "tolerated" in New England and Virginia, not made welcome on neutral or common ground. In particular the Act of Toleration had excluded Roman Catholics; therefore American Catholics in Maryland and elsewhere suffered for a century a "penal period" in their history. New England (with the exception of Rhode Island) and Virginia came up to the Revolution, therefore, with the idea of a state church as part of their heritage from the Old World and their continued practice in the New World. Why was it, then, that with the drafting of our Constitution this whole age-old idea of a state church vanished from our mind, so that it is today little more than a matter of forgotten ancient history?

The reasons are many. The most obvious is this: Massachusetts would never agree to an Episcopal establishment; Virginia would never agree to a Congregational establishment. Each cancelled the other. As for the other colonies, such as Rhode Island and Pennsylvania, sectarians had won a permanent place for themselves there, and the very idea of any establishment whatsoever was repugnant to them. The German pietist groups in Pennsylvania had only bitter memories of state churches. By the middle of the eighteenth century even the Quakers had begun to withdraw from too much direct participation in public affairs, fearing the compromises which attend too close identification with "the world." In Rhode Island, Roger Williams had preached from the first absolute separation of church and state, and the Baptists were a rapidly growing group in all the colonies.

But beyond all this the makers of the American Constitution were men who were influenced mainly by the tide of liberal opinion that was rising here as in England. John Locke set the pattern for their thinking. They were men of the "Enlightenment," their religion seems to have been that which is vaguely known as Deism. They believed in a creator of the world, in the moral order of the universe, in homage to be duly paid to the creator and his works in creation, as in the simple ethical teachings of Jesus. But their God left them largely to their own devices, bidding their hearts "vibrate to the iron string" of self-reliance. The Calvinistic theology of New England was already in process of dissolution. The Episcopal churches of Virginia were largely shorn of effective leadership, since most of the more prominent clergy had gone back to England. Ecclesiastics, whether Congregational or Episcopalian, enjoyed only a fraction of the influence they had previously exerted on public affairs. The New England churches were further weakened by interior theological controversies. New ideas of the nature of man, wholly alien to the premises of Calvinism, were the order of the day.

John Locke's *Epistles on Toleration* were by this time supplemented by Rousseau's reflections on religion and morality, as proposed in his *Contrat Social*. Thus one of our historians says that "The new republic was born in as secular a spirit as the later French republic"; while another writer adds,

The whole atmosphere of the entire literature is secular. . . . The republic's ablest statesmen saw fit to ignore the whole subject of religion. It is not that it is attacked, or made little of, but the fact is that it is entirely ignored. The purely negative character of this attitude appears on the face of the instrument.

Sectarians joined with political revolutionists in celebrating the ideal of Liberty, and translating it into achieved fact. In church matters devotion to this ideal meant the repudiation of the whole theory of a state church. So far as the state was concerned James Madison must have voiced the convictions and the common sense of his contemporaries when he said that a multitude of religious denominations was probably the best practical safeguard of the principle of religious liberty. While the Constitution is, therefore, an instrument which is predominantly secular in its character, that secularity had its warrant in the determination of the founding fathers to guarantee to all alike their religious liberties.

Separation of church and state in America was a federal fact from 1789-1791. Local establishments lingered on in

New England for some years thereafter. Connecticut continued support of its Congregational churches, in the form of public money applied to clergy stipends, until 1818; New Hampshire until 1819. The last vestiges of a state church disappeared from the American scene in 1833 when Orthodox Congregationalists demurred at paying further taxes for the support of such of their original churches as had become Unitarian. The American stage was thus set for what has become the familiar and generally accepted pattern for our corporate religious life—denominationalism.

II

Let us come to close quarters, then, with the present fact. The estimated population of the United States is at present 134,000,000. The "inclusive" church membership of the country is estimated as 67,300,000. This figure presupposes formal membership on the part of adults, but includes also children in the families. This is half of our population.

Figures for church membership are notoriously unreliable. In this instance they should be, perhaps, written off by 50 per cent so far as active participation and regular attendance are concerned. But the fact remains that, nominally, the country is one half churched and the other half unchurched. The figures at least mean that the 67,300,000 persons included on church rolls are aware of church backgrounds in their family history, and probably turn to the church for rites of baptism, marriage, and burial. In these respects America is less secularized than Europe and our *mores* still require the words of religion said on the high occasions of birth, marriage, and death. On the other hand we may not dismiss the unchurched half of our population as being aggressively anticlerical and irreligious. One of the recent popular polls reports 90 per cent of our people as believing in the existence of God. Emancipated intellectuals are a familiar commonplace in our academic and professional circles. They are, however, a minority of our population. There is still in our people as a whole a residual feeling for religion, and much of that temper which *The Soldier in Arms* of the last war called the "inarticulate religion" of the average man. Meanwhile the churches, so far as formal figures are concerned, are not losing ground rapidly, as we so often suppose. From 1930 to 1942 our population increased 9.1 per cent, while church membership during that same period increased 12.9 per cent. The church may be dying, as we are so often told, but like Browning's martyr she can at least say, "I was some time a-dying." As any hard-headed politician knows, the church vote in America is a factor which may not safely be ignored.

The inclusive church membership of 67,300,000 is divided as follows: Protestant, 38,500,000; Roman Catholic, 23,000,000; Jewish, 4,600,000; Eastern Orthodox, 1,200,-000.

We are concerned in this volume with the diversities and divisions of these persons into 256 independent denominations. For the purposes of our inquiry the Roman Catholic Church, much the largest and most massive single "denomination" we have, counts as a single denomination. The fact that it counts as only "one" out of 256 is, of course, a wholly inaccurate and misleading account of its proportional prominence and influence. It is more than twice as strong as any other denomination. Its case is to be stated in a later chapter by Father LaFarge.

The Jews publish no religious statistics. They hold in theory that the people of Israel as a whole is the congregation, therefore the figures for Jewish church membership are those for our Jewish population as a whole. In practice the Jews are divided into Orthodox, Conservative, and Liberal groups. As far as one can determine, these three types of synagogue compass in actual fact about half the Jews in the country; the ratio of church membership is therefore that for the population as a whole. Meanwhile the Jews, like the Catholics, comprise a single denomination only. President Finkelstein is to interpret these facts and figures in a subsequent chapter.

The Eastern Orthodox Churches are all European in origin, coming from Russia, Greece, Bulgaria, and the like. That church, here as in the Old World, is a "commonwealth" of churches, each identified in the country of its origin with the state. In our census they reappear as eleven independent denominations. Therefore, Roman Catholicism, Judaism, and Eastern Orthodoxy account for thirteen of our denominations, though they include 28,800,000 of our church members. These figures leave 38,500,000 of our church members to be divided among 243 Protestant denominations.

It is in this area, therefore, that the problem, and, if you will, the scandal of prodigal denominationalism, as we know it in America, is most vividly stated and most acutely felt. Professor McNeill is to tell us hereafter what is now being done to help solve the problem. His later words may be, however, prefaced by some account of the initial facts.

The Protestant churches of the United States are divided into two fairly distinct types: the larger denominations which retain some kind of family identity; the smaller "sects" (so called, though as we have already said that term has no strict relevance here) which live a life apart. These latter groups are a characteristic product of our culture, but are very much in the minority. The figures indicate that of our 243 Protestant denominations at least 200 must be classed as "small sects," each with a membership of less than 50,000, many of them showing only 2,000 to 3,000 members. These 200 small sects include only 3 per cent of our total church membership.

Some of these groups are surviving forms of pietist movements of the sixteenth and seventeenth centuries, transplanted here in Colonial times. That is particularly true of our small and religiously "isolationist" German denominations such as the Mennonites, the Schwenkfelders, the Hutterian Brethren. So, also, the Plymouth Brethren, who came to us from England a century ago, number only 25,000 members; but that relatively small total has been divided and subdivided into eight recognized denominations. Most of these older sects are found in agricultural areas and live a frugal and economically substantial life, self-respecting and respected by their neighbors round.

Others of the smaller sects, and these are in the majority, have sprung from this soil, often among underprivileged persons of our own native stock. They may be found in pockets of the mountains and in the dreary slums of our cities. Their religion is frankly escapist, an emotional compensation for lives sunk in drabness and dullness. There is far more interest in celebration of the joys of heaven, in the prospect of some apocalyptic day of the Lord when the existing order shall be overthrown, than in the gradual amelioration of things as they now are.

At the extreme left are movements led by picturesque persons like Aimée McPherson and Father Divine, whose sensational methods are calculated to beat the Devil at his own game in Los Angeles or Harlem. Many of these "denominations" are short-lived, depending for their vitality upon some single vivid founder, a vitality which instantly wanes with a second generation. Each, however ephemeral, is recognized by the census and protected by law. Before the impartial tribunal of government such sects enjoy all the rights and privileges accorded to the larger historic bodies. They make little or no contribution to the corporate religious life of the country, since most of them deny the validity of the more conventional churches and refuse to coöperate with them. Each plays a lone hand, and, all together, because of their individualistic and unworldly piety, stand apart from serious social effort. They furnish, however, fascinating subject matter for study by the historian, the theologian, and the sociologist. We see here how religious movements are born out of ecstatic experiences, how primitive groups are organized, and how churches "cool off" with the passage of time, either to die away or to grow up into a sobriety that can endure.

When we turn to the major family groups within Protestantism the figures break down as follows:

Baptist (19 denominations)	11,400,000
Methodist (19 denominations)	8,400,000
Lutheran (20 denominations)	4,000,000
Presbyterian (10 denominations)	2,800,000
Protestant Episcopal (a single denomination)	2,100,000
Disciples of Christ (a single denomination)	1,700,000
Congregational Christian (a single denomination)	1,100,000
	31,500,000

As for the denominations listed in the family groups above, certain generalizations may be made. With the exception of the Disciples of Christ, all hark back to European origins, and, since the Disciples represent a modified Presbyterianism, even that body cannot be credited to us as a significant innovation. The Baptist and Methodist groups include a large number of our Negro churches, the Baptists being in the great majority. The largest single Protestant body in the country is now the Methodist Church, with a membership of 7,400,000.

There have been some theological schisms within our older churches over the last hundred and fifty years, but far fewer than one might have expected. The general "liberal" movement of the late eighteenth and early nineteenth centuries divided the historic Congregational Church of New England into its Orthodox and Unitarian bodies. A similar movement divided the Society of Friends into Orthodox and Hicksites. So also the Old Light and New Light controversy within Presbyterianism. This issue between liberalism and conservatism still remains unresolved. It rests mainly upon the two rival doctrines of man which are at stake. Is man a fallen creature who can be saved only by the grace of God, or is he a morally ascending creature trusting in no small part to the virtue of self-reliance for his salvation? The issue is as old as St. Augustine and Pelagius, but still persists.

One of the most baffling phenomena of American life is the survival in the extreme orthodox churches of the elder and more disparaging doctrines of man, which are given lip service Sunday by Sunday, while the business of the other six days is nominally conducted upon the supposition that man can make something of himself. It is strange that there has been little or no felt inconsistency in this paradox. The working religion of the six weekdays in our American culture has plainly been "liberal." We think well of ourselves as human raw material and we think that by our own effort we can become better, both in our own persons and in the persons of our children. A pioneer has to be self-reliant, and our history thus far has been, until most recent times, that of a succession of pioneers. It is only within most recent times that we have had occasion to question our axiomatic liberalism. Man is not giving as good an account of himself, the world over, as the theory would seem to require. The biological sciences, witness Huxley, have always had a perverse interest in something like Calvinism; the newer psychology does not give a reassuring account of the underworld in the individual, and as for the world as a whole we are being told in many quarters that the last of the sands are now running out in the hourglass of our kind of civilization. We have not yet become illiberal, nor do we seriously propose to become so, but the rhetoric of the late eighteenth century is not as romantic and compelling today as it once was. In the main, however, our major religious bodies have not been seriously divided by theological controversies. That may be because we are an active rather than a contemplative people.

Such major schisms as we have had were occasioned by the slavery issue. In the middle of the last century that sore subject divided the Methodist, Baptist, and Presbyterian denominations into Northern and Southern churches. The two halves of the Methodist Church reunited a few years ago to become a single body. The Baptist and Presbyterian churches are still divided. It is significant, however, that these breaches were occasioned not by theological or ecclesiastical differences, but by the rival cultures and economies of pre-Civil War days. Slavery may have been, indeed was, a moral issue, but its statement at the time implied identification with either the industrial North or the cotton-growing South. In the main, therefore, our American churches have not been greatly agitated by theological controversies, and most of the larger denominations have survived intact whatever differences of belief have appeared within their borders.

To the historic diversity of churches and sects which we inherited from Europe we have contributed only two movements which may be called substantial ecclesiastical innovations: Christian Science and Mormonism. Both the Church of Christ, Scientist, and the Church of the Latter Day Saints have become familiar and stable societies. They are assured of survival here, in so far as any church has such assurance, and each is an active missionary denomination, spreading its gospel all over the world.

Of the smaller denominations, the Unitarians and the

Quakers have had and still have an influence out of all proportion to their numbers. They pioneer boldly in the realms of faith and practice. They are not the "lump" of American Protestantism, but have done much to leaven the lump. The genial doctrine of man with which Unitarianism cast its lot a hundred and twenty-five years ago is now tacitly, if not formally, accepted in many of our Protestant churches. The Society of Friends has done much to defend the rights of conscience which the Reformation proposed to vindicate, and to reanimate that "agonized conscience" which Santayana once said was the heart of Puritanism.

III

What, now, can be said in conclusion as to our religious situation in its entirety? The following generalizations are tentatively proposed.

1. The separation of church and state prevents our government, at all of its levels, from identifying itself with any single form of faith and practice. We have no official religion. William Temple, the late Archbishop of Canterbury, said not long before his death that it was the office of Lambeth (the London residence of the Archbishop) to remind Westminster of its duty to God. There is no American churchman who can claim officially any such right, and the assumption of such a right would be universally regarded as an impertinence. Churchmen often speak openly on matters of national or local policy, but they do so as individuals.

We have chaplains in our Army and Navy, chaplains for our Congress and our legislatures. We exempt church property used for religious purposes from taxation. We defend public worship against nuisances. Presidents and governors make public proclamations giving thanks to God for blessings past and invoking his guidance for the future. All this is true. Yet the name of God does not occur in the Constitution, though there have been many attempts to get it inserted. The state holds at the best a position of benevolent neutrality and cannot commit itself on any specific matters of religious faith and practice. We have delivered ourselves from the unedifying conflicts between church and state which litter the pages of history in other lands. We have perhaps saved religion and thus the church from countless unhappy compromises and to this extent kept our religion "unspotted from the world," but we have denied the state the right and duty to speak to us in the name of God.

2. In particular we have denied all state-supported institutions of education, from the common school to the university, an opportunity to give religious instruction to each oncoming generation. In some of the lower schools, where there is a homogeneous community, minimal practices are allowed, but these practices consist at the most of non-controversial readings from the Bible and an occasional hymn. There may be a prayer offered at a high school graduation or a baccalaureate sermon (more often called an "address") preached at a state university commencement. But that is as far as the state can go, and ventures which go even that far often get into difficulty. Thus the papers have just reported a Jewish rabbi who resigned his post because his congregation was willing to tolerate the singing of Christian Christmas carols in the public schools of his community.

Bible reading often comes to legal grief over the distinction between the Protestant King James version and the Catholic Douai version.

Therefore the task of passing on the great religious traditions in our culture devolves upon the home and the Sunday School. In days past private devotions and parental instruction were a commonplace in the American home; today they are the exception. Sunday Schools, likewise, for reasons which are by no means clear, are falling off rather rapidly in enrollment, probably because in the minds of both parents and children they suffer by contrast with day schools in their standards and methods. Apparently, also, the mounting burden of "home work" carrying over from the day school monopolizes more and more of a child's Sunday hours. In any case the self-imposed restrictions under which the state operates, and the declining effectiveness of the average home and church as teaching centers, are breeding up a generation of religious illiterates among us, with whom we are only too familiar in school and college. It is not that our youth is irreligious, rather it is a-religious, non-religious. But we are faced with the fact that, at present more than at any time in the past, there is a cultural break in the continuity of the religious traditions of our people. Our days are no longer "bound each to each by natural piety," in so far as that piety is expressed in historic forms.

3. American culture has been hitherto predominantly individualistic. It is true that the forms of that culture are now apparently in process of passing away. Some rejoice in the change, some regret it. Either way the religious life of the country as a whole is, in this respect, in arrears of the

rest of our life. Our churches are still living in the afterglow of "states' rights" at a time when federalization is the order of the day.

This fact is substantiated by the very large percentage of American churches organized on the "congregational" polity, i.e., the independence and, up to a point, the theoretical self-sufficiency, of the individual parish church. Of our 256 denominations 99 are organized on a congregational or near-congregational polity. No such situation obtains in any other land, or has ever obtained in the past. This polity undoubtedly fitted the pioneer period of our history admirably, when western frontiersmen had to take the conduct of affairs into their own hands without waiting for instructions from some eastern hinterland. Indeed, so native and necessary was that conception of the church to our earlier life that the tempers of congregationalism communicated themselves to other denominations of a more centralized type. Thus, the Bishop of Gloucester, a friendly but candid critic of American affairs, has often said that, from the standpoint of a European, all American churches are congregational.

There is, therefore, a patent "lag" between a national life which, in matters political, economic, and industrial, is becoming more and more centralized and standardized, and the conventional "congregational"—i.e., individualistic—temper of our church life. We have no recognized forms for the expression of corporate religious convictions and common moral principles to serve the kind of culture which environs us today. We lay siege to legislatures and governments with our petitions and recommendations, solemnly passed in our several assemblies, but these pronouncements are still "denominational" and often cancel each other. The only political power we actually exercise is exercised by us individually at the polls.

This restriction of religion to the area of individual concern is, of course, one of the consequences of the separation of church and state. Churches are, from the standpoint of the American state, private societies voluntarily organized and maintained. Legally they are on a par with countless other societies similarly organized. Over most of the centuries of our era organized religion has never found itself in this condition. Established churches have received, in the nature of the case, recognition and influence—whether for better or for worse is for the historian to say—denied our denominations. Sects have either been at the worst candidly "harried"—to quote James I—or at the best socially unclassed. In the former instance organized religion speaks with an authority denied our denominations; in the latter instance it has the vitality we associate with all vigorous minority movements. Our American denominations are denied either the complacent voice of authority or the strident note of dissent. Our religious equalitarianism, as it obtains among our many "voluntary associations," deprives our denominations both of the present weight of the one voice and of the possible promise of the other voice. We have instead an undistinguished babel of voices lacking at the one extreme the accredited tones of a "church" and at the other the sharp accent of a "sect."

4. In a time of war we agree not to stress our religious differences and try to work together as amicably as possible. But there is no denying the actual and radical differences of faith and conduct which obtain between our many de-

nominations. There is little gain, for the sake of some specious and superficial unity, in pretending that they do not exist and are not important. The familiar cliché, "It doesn't matter what a man believes, as long as he tries to live rightly," is the counsel either of indifference or of despair. It does matter what a man believes, since his conduct is conditioned by his beliefs and his character is formed by those beliefs. Thomas Huxley was much nearer the mark when he said, "The most sacred act of man's life is to say and to feel, 'I believe thus and thus to be so.' All the greatest rewards and all the heaviest penalties of existence cling about that act."

The differences between Judaism and Christianity, between Catholicism and Protestantism, between Fundamentalism and Liberalism are both actual and important. They involve rival views of the being and character of God, the structure of the universe, the nature of man, the processes of history, the conduct of life. Each has its warrant and each has its worth. The intuitions and instinctive judgments which prompt them are more important than the rational processes by which men attempt subsequently to buttress them.

As one ponders the course of religious history one finds everywhere, either in the open or beneath, a fictitious unity, a clash of temperaments. The priest and the prophet are two distinct types. The religion of the Old Testament is divided between them and their differences were never fully reconciled and resolved. The Sons of Mary and the Sons of Martha vie with each other for priority in the Christian tradition, if not for a monopoly of that tradition. The contemplative and the active types have their once-removed expression in our religious institutions. It would be folly for religion to attempt to go behind or go around what seem to be primal psychological data.

In the broad sense of the word our churches represent two different directions in religion: that from God to man and that from man to God; the deductive and the inductive; the objective and the subjective; the dogmatic and the empirical. Thus, in an attempt to give freshness to terms that have perhaps become so trite that they have lost their meaning, the Edinburgh Conference on Faith and Order described the two stubbornly persistent types of church as "authoritarian" and "personal." Theoretically, each needs the other to complement it; practically each of us inclines by temperament, heredity, and tradition to one or the other of these types and chooses, or is born into, his church accordingly. This antinomy is a given initial fact in human nature. According to Jung it provides the first and best test for distinguishing between man and man. It has, and in the nature of the case must have, its expression in the life of corporate groups. Unity should be achieved not by denying these initial differences, but by comprehending them. Without forfeiting the truth of his own native insights every churchman ought to be willing to concede the possible validity of the position of the party of the other part. The practical difficulty is that few persons seem able to do so without feeling that they have turned state's evidence against their own convictions.

The problem of religious unity—and in institutional terms this means church unity—is a genuine one, important and stubborn. Nothing will be gained by genial indifferentism. By virtue of our denominationalism, as against a church-sect pattern for our corporate religious life, America has given the fullest and freest opportunity for the statement of the problem. By the same token, since freedom from the dictates of the state leaves the field open for unlimited trial and error in these matters, it may well be that America will be able to work out some solution of the problem of religious unity prohibited believers who must operate within more rigid limits.

The solution of the problem is not yet in sight. The task of the present is that of constant informal commerce between religious persons of radically different traditions. There must be much more patient and constant visiting back and forth across the party walls of denominationalism. This can be done because ultimately there is in the American temperament "something that doesn't love a wall." We have pretty well exhausted the possibilities of intensive self-culture in our several denominations. We have heard enough liturgical "Amens" to our own creeds and confessions to pamper our self-assurance. We are increasingly aware that we need the correction of an antithetical half-truth to save our own half-truth from dying of inbreeding. But this awareness exists as yet mainly in individuals and small groups, who will have to pioneer across party lines in advance of the laggard societies they represent. That is the immediate task for all men of religious good will in America. Our religious freedom, which was first a right, now takes on the sterner aspect of a religious duty, not merely for the sake of the unity and integrity of our own American life, but in behalf of the divided peoples of the wider world.

IV

Finally, these several facts and scattered reflections should leave us in no doubt as to the problematical nature of any possible "national religion." Benjamin Franklin said that religion is a personal matter which a man does not wish to discuss with others. There is among us still a good deal of just this proper reticence, which may however be abused in terms of selfishness, bigotry, or plain indifference. The state meanwhile decrees that any and all churches are at the most "private associations." Our institutional religious life is therefore ordered on the "social contract" theory, stated in a multitude of concrete instances. This decreed privacy limits the activities of even the largest and most powerful of our religious bodies. When they transgress its legal limits they find themselves in trouble. How to translate the religious reticences of the single individual and the statutory privacy of the single denomination into the terms of what Josiah Royce called "A Beloved Community of Memory and Hope" is a problem which our Constitution does not help us solve in the terms of any single "American religion." Indeed, despite the great blessings it has vouchsafed us in the terms of our religious liberties, the Constitution seems at times to render a clear solution remote, if not impossible.

NOTE: Parts of this chapter have been condensed from longer chapters in a volume on *Religion in America*, to be published in the near future by the Cambridge University Press in England, and later republished in the United States by the Macmillan Company.

John LaFarge, S.J.

❖ 2 ❖

Roman Catholicism

A COLORED soldier now in India wrote to me recently: "I never appreciated what unity meant until yesterday when I went to Mass in a Calcutta church and knelt there with all those strange new folks." The world today is appreciating as never before the importance of unity in every phase of life. Our politicians are deeply concerned about party unity, our labor leaders seek it in the field of trade unionism. We treasure every evidence of unity between the big powers in guaranteeing security, and religious forces strive for the unity of all nations in laying a juridical foundation of world peace. Last but not least, the souls of men are clamoring for religious unity.

For unity is a dynamic thing. The ancient philosophers placed unity among the transcendentals, on a par with the good, the true, and the beautiful, and we know that as a political and social agent the appeal to unity is all-powerful. I remember the oppression I experienced a year before the war as I looked out of the train window on entering Germany and saw in a broad, sunny field the words blazoned on a large white wooden cross: *Ein Volk, ein Reich, ein*

Führer! Unity is the glorious attribute of the Most High which we proclaim with ecstasy in the Apostles' and the Nicene Creeds. It is the grinding thought-tool of the most terrible tyrants the world has ever seen.

Without religious unity we have no safeguard against that distortion of unity which we call totalitarianism. However much we may differ as to the form which religious unity should take, all are agreed as to the terrible evil of disunity and division in the field of religion. The most solemn prayer of the founder of the Christian religion, the prayer uttered on the eve of his Sacred Passion, was the plea to the Heavenly Father "That they all may be one, as thou Father in me, and I in Thee" (John 17: 21).

Any discussion, however, of this Christian ideal must necessarily be preceded by a survey of the various concepts of unity itself. If religious unity implies any relationship to the Catholic Church, obviously a primary task would be to form some idea of what may be the Catholic's own idea and concept of religious unity.

In the following lines I am not endeavoring to write an essay on the Catholic theology of religious unity, but merely to point out one or two thoughts in this connection which may be helpful to men of good will who are aware of the appalling harm done in the world by religious disunity. I shall present first a very brief summary of what might be called the traditional Catholic statement on the subject of church unity, before discussing at greater length certain features in the Catholic's concept of unity which may present a repellent feature to the modern mind.

II

It is commonly stated by modern Catholic theologians that church unity has a twofold aspect, one which is internal and mystical, one which is external and visible. The internal or mystical unity of the church is none other than the mystical body of Christ. The principle of that unity is the vivifying spirit of Christ himself. It is illustrated in the recent Encyclical of Pope Pius XII, *Mystici Corporis* (Nos. 76 and 77):

Hence, this word in its correct signification gives us to understand that the Church, a perfect society of its kind, is not made up of merely moral and juridical elements and principles. It is far superior to all other human societies; it surpasses them as grace surpasses nature, as things immortal are above all those that perish. Such human societies, and in the first place Civil Society, are by no means to be despised or belittled. But the Church in its entirety is not found within this natural order, any more than the whole of man is encompassed within the organism of our mortal body.

The juridical principles, on which also the Church rests and is established, derive from the Divine constitution given to it by Christ, and contribute to attaining its super-natural end; but what lifts the society of Christians far, far above the whole natural order is the Spirit of our Redeemer, who until the end of time penetrates every part of the Church's being and is active within it. He is the source of every grace and every gift and every miraculous power. Just as our composite mortal body, for all its being a marvelous work of the Creator, falls far short of the eminent dignity of our soul, so the social structure of the Christian community, though eloquent of its Divine Architect's wisdom, remains still something inferior, when compared to the spiritual gifts which give it beauty and life and to their Divine source.

The principle of the external unity of the church is the Petrine-Apostolic ministry; and it appears in a threefold aspect:

Unity of faith, which consists in the common profession by all members of the church of one and the same faith, as proposed by one and the same teaching authority. Such a unity of faith demands not only that all the members give inward assent to the doctrines proposed by the infallible teaching authority, but also that they express this assent externally by some outward form of profession. It implies, furthermore, a *total* unity of faith which extends to all revealed doctrine (to certain doctrines explicitly and to the whole body of doctrine implicitly). Such unity of faith is not destroyed by dissensions of theologians, as long as they honestly adhere to the definitive definitions of the teaching authority, nor is it destroyed by the process of developing the full doctrinal implications of matters already held to by faith.

Unity of government, which consists in the obedience rendered by the faithful to one and the same supreme spiritual authority instituted by Jesus Christ. This authority reposes primarily in the Roman pontiff towards whom, in the words of the Vatican Council, all the members of the church "both pastors and faithful of whatsoever rite or dignity, both pastors and faithful, individually and collectively, are bound by the duty of hierarchic subordination and true obedience not merely in matters of faith and morals, but also in those which pertain to the discipline and government of the Church throughout the world." (Vat. Coun. Sess. IV. Dogm. Const. on the Church of Christ. Cpt. 3.) The Bishops, too, share in this governing authority, inasmuch as collectively gathered in an ecumenical council they have jurisdiction over the universal church, subject however to the authority of the Pope, and individually each has jurisdiction over his own diocese.

A third type of external unity of the church is *unity of fellowship* (communion, *koinonia*). The object of this unity is the union of all the faithful amongst one another. It may be called the social unity of the church, which flows from the very concept of a society. From such a social unity will follow that no members of the church, none of its constituent communities, will be totally independent of it either in their existence or their mode of operation. They are all part of one and the same social and mystical body. It effects a fundamental unity of religious sacrifice, of the sacraments, and a basic unity of purpose in every part of the church, but it is not destroyed by a legitimate variety of rites in the church so long as their diversity does not affect the substance of the worship instituted by Christ. Nor is it affected by the diversity of disciplinary laws which are adapted to different times and places and persons as the case may be.

Certain striking aspects, which might be called the "phenomenal" Catholic Church, illustrate each aspect of the church's external unity. Unity of faith is made particularly visible by the church's creeds, her definitions, and her visible teaching authority of the papacy and the hierarchy. Unity of government is evident from the world prominence of the successor of St. Peter, Vicar of Christ, whom all Catholics acknowledge as their leader and pastor. Her unity of government is particularly notable in times of a general ecumenical council. The social unity of the church at once strikes the eye in the ordinary daily contact with the Catholic faith: with the Catholic organism as it impinges upon the daily life of an American citizen; in the whole complex of diocesan and parish organization, her schools of education, parochial societies, of the works of the press, charity, her ministry, her missions, etc.

III

It is this third aspect, the social aspect of the church, its "phenomenal" fellowship or *koinonia*, which has been the object recently of particularly close attention on the part of non-Catholic critics. To consider the picture of Catholic unity which is implied in some of their descriptions it might seem to have two outstanding characteristics.

In the first place, it presents a front, as it were, against diversity, whether of worship, or of religious doctrine, or of personal moral and ascetic ideals. Unity of fellowship, in such a picture, might seem to be identified with uniformity, so that a test of the true Catholic character of any phase or manifestation of its social unity would seem to be its increased approach to complete uniformity in worship, thought, and manners. Uniformity, however, is a different thing from unity, for unity is only then fully realized when in some manner it contains a provision for diversity.

A second repelling feature in such a portrait of the Catholic concept of unity would be the semblance of an exclusively objective character, as something lacking the implication of personal, creative action on the part of man. The individual, in this supposition, merely fits himself into the system as best he may. Unity then would be settled from above: in the strict sense as a creation of the hierarchy, who would decide among themselves what kind of unified organization they see fit to sanction upon earth, think out what will work best, what will best attain the various ends or purposes they have in mind, and say then to the individual:

Look, here it is written in the Catechism. Take our plan and adapt yourself to it. If you discover it has no relation to your own personal life and personal problems, this is simply a matter for regret. But our plan is thus and so, and it is your job to adjust yourself to it in whatever way you may find possible.

Both such concepts, then—of all-out uniformity and of complete objectification—would seem to militate against the general acceptability of any doctrine of religious unity which would embody them. But does a closer examination of the church's teaching and practice in the matter of unity bear out the assumption that such is the correct statement of the Catholic position?

IV

If Catholic teaching on religious unity enjoined the rigid uniformity which has just been described, it would be hard to reconcile it with the actual social teaching of the church. Even where the church's social teaching deals with matters of the temporal order, not with the purely religious or supernatural, it would be hardly possible that so radical a contrast should exist between the two sets of doctrines. The question of the reconciliation of unity and diversity in the social order has occupied the thought of Catholic social teaching during recent years. The problems of nationalism and of racism have brought it to the fore and are calculated to emphasize it still more in the immediate future. The church's reaction to totalitarianism with its process of making all men uniform has been to assert the organic diversified concept of society. Nowhere do we find this more fully developed than in the first Encyclical, *Summi Pontificatus*, of the present Pope:

A marvelous vision, which makes us see the human race in the unity of one common origin in God "one God and Father of all, Who is above all, and through all, and in us all" (Ephesians 4: 6); in the unity of nature which in every man is equally composed of material body and spiritual, immortal soul; in the unity of the immediate end and mission in the world; in the unity of dwelling place, the earth, of whose resources all men can by natural right avail themselves, to sustain and develop life; in the unity of the supernatural end, God Himself, to Whom all should tend; in the unity of means to secure that end.

From whatever aspect we view the social and political organism, whether it be the horizontal or the vertical, we find the Catholic Church deeply enamored of the idea of a wide diversity of functions, of tastes, of national characteristics, in short, of all the things that make up the richness and variety of human life as comprehended in the idea of unity. This broad view of human society is no accident, no mere accommodation to passing circumstances, but flows from the inner concept of the church itself. Diversity is not a mere concession to circumstances, a sort of weakness in the application of unity to human circumstances, but proceeds from the very concept of the church as the church of the entire human race. For the Catholic Church is simply another way of saying the church of all mankind, the church which represents the extension in time and space of the incarnation of the Son of God.

Hence its note of diversity is not a mere adornment to a solid pillar of unity, but is of the very texture of unity, part of the scheme itself.

One can readily grant that the diversified aspect of the church, owing to historic circumstances, may in many cases be considerably obscured. Uniformization is a precise reaction to a rupture of Christian unity. Wherever that unity is disrupted there will grow in the remaining part a tendency to a certain rigidity of self-defense. Such an example is the popular concept of the Eastern Churches and the Church Catholic. In the minds of a great many people, for instance, the church is identified with the Latin Rite. The Latin language is frequently designated as the language of the Church Universal, yet the Latin language only in a qualified sense is the language of the Catholic Church. It is the language of the major part of the Church Universal as it now exists, and in the present conditions of things the missionary development of the church is overwhelmingly associated with the Latin Rite. The same would apply to the nationalistic aspect which is apt to befall sections of the church when certain large nations have departed from her central unity. Those national elements who remain united to the central body will be identified with the Church

Universal both in their own minds and very often in the minds of the people that dislike them. For the Russian, for instance, the Catholic Church is the Polish Church; and for the Hussites, it was the Church of the Habsburgs. To many Americans in this country the Catholic Church until recent years was regarded as the church of the Irish; for the Yankee pioneer of the Southwest, the church of the "greaser"; or for the Negro Baptist or Methodist, the white man's church, and so on. The occasions for such beliefs are evident. But they are popular misconceptions and are not an expression of the church's own mind. They are the result of human weakness, often occasioned by the inability of the church's own members to grasp the tremendous implications of immense diversity in unity which is a divine and stupendous thing and beyond unaided human power to realize and put into effect.

v

So, far from being true that unity and diversity in the church are opposing forces, it is much more correct to say that they both spring from the same source. The unity of the church is not the result of coalition; it is not an effect of compromise in some form of super-organization. The creed of the church is not to be compared to the resolutions of a debating society. It is rather, as observed by Johannes Moehler, correct to say that the common expressions which translate this unity into language arise spontaneously from a common source and are not the result of the deliberation of individuals who wish to indicate by an exterior sign their decision of uniting themselves in some form of a new society. "The Church," says Moehler, "did not decide the universal adoption of the Seven Sacraments in order to express and maintain its unity of worship among all its differences." Rather, the church recognized "that among all the Rites which it practiced, these Seven Sacraments were directly attached to the will of the Saviour and formed one of the essential armatures of its organism." [1] As was recently stated by a commentator on these words of Moehler: "The formulae defined by the Church do not represent an attempt to realize the unity of thought but they are the spontaneous reaction of faith in the face of error which denies them." I may be pardoned if I quote a little further from the same commentator (Father Yves de Montcheuil, S.J., former Professor of Theology in Lyons, murdered recently by the Nazis for his ministrations to people of other nationalities and beliefs, *L'Eglise est Une*, p. 246 sq.):

An important conclusion may be derived from this manner of understanding the appearance of the external expressions of unity. The true bond of diversity is not to be found in that which they contain in common. If "oppositions" in the Church do not turn into "contradictions" this is not because of those elements of identity which are found in them everywhere. To entertain that idea would be to engage in a misunderstanding as to the nature of the common elements and the nature of the different elements. The common elements, necessary as they are, constitute a wholly external expression of profound unity: they cannot be its reason and its source. The different elements are not juxtaposed upon the common elements according to each person's preference. They have the same origin even if they have a different function. One cannot say that common

[1] J. A. Moehler, *Die Einheit in der Kirche*, § 40.

life is expressed by that which is identical in worship and doctrine and practical morals and in individuality, and individuality by that which is found to be different. In point of fact, everything comes from the same profound source. The true bond between diversities is found in the unity of the life which engenders them. This is to be asserted with regard both to the different parts of the Church in one and the same epoch and with regard to successive periods in the Church's life.

VI

Hence it is that for the Catholic the attempt to create unity by a process of adjustment, conference, organization, or reconciliation or whatever one may call it between the points of view of different churches is something entirely out of agreement with his concept of the unity of the church itself. The Catholic is conscious that this may place him in the position of seeming to be reactionary, an exclusivist, a narrow-minded person. But his position does not come from any yearning to be exclusive, a desire to appropriate religious truth exclusively to himself. He has no desire to be standing on an eminence and say, I am holier than thou; on the contrary, he recognizes in the personal lives of countless individuals outside of his church people who are far better than he is, to whom he looks up with utmost respect. In many he sees a more finely developed spiritual nature. He is aware that according to their own lights, according to their own abilities they have apprehended many a spiritual truth which has escaped him. The very spiritual privations which they undergo have aroused in them a keenness and hunger which may, to his shame, be lacking in him who has taken much for granted that God has provided bounteously to him from his own table. All these add up to a matter of self-reproach but do not in any way obviate the complete difference of point of view.

For one who looks upon religion as something to be built up from a multitude of various individual revelations and conflicting doctrines, there is nothing particularly alarming about a statement such as that made by John D. Rockefeller a few days ago when he insisted to the Protestant Council of the City of New York that we are all going to heaven in different ways, that creeds and dogmas do not count; that his reborn church would cut through the barriers of conflicting rituals and formalities, and so on. To the Catholic mind such an utterance is devastating, not, as I have just said, because of any natural exclusiveness on his part, but because it contradicts the basic nature of that unity and diversity which to him springs from the very inmost thoughts of the Christian Revelation. The unity of the church for the Catholic is simply the unity of humanity itself remade or regenerated in Christ through his reconciliation with the Father. To confuse that unity, to dissolve its inmost character by identifying it with the merely human process of rationalization and synthesis, is to destroy the essence of redemption itself, to destroy that inmost bond of union which is God's free gift to individuals and to humanity at large through the incarnation and the redemption. The church's unity of doctrine and government and unity in its social body are simply the visible pledge of the reality of its union with the Saviour himself. They are a visible and tangible sign that the church is carrying out on earth that mission which the Redeemer entrusted to her, that mission which is the fulfillment of his design to offer to the entire human race the opportunity of incorporation into the glory of God. [2]

VII

Passing, then, to the second difficulty we may ask: but is this not too objective, too non-individual, too non-creative a concept? Where does the individual come in? If he cannot create unity by adjustment and synthesis, how does he create it? Is it again something simply given to him, simply imposed upon him that he is obliged to take, or is it something that he makes himself, in some form or other? The Catholic Church rejects that type of ecumenism which in reality is merely an attempt to realize a "federation of schisms"; but in doing so does this mean some impairment of the activity of the creative function of the individual?

My answer to this is decisive. Far from neglecting the individual, the moral aspect of the Catholic concept of unity resolves itself into the problem of the individual, for it is the individual himself who expresses it and upon whose coöperation its realization ultimately depends.

This may be seen both as a privilege and as a burden.

As a privilege, it is the dignity of the individual that unity cannot be imposed upon him by any force, even that of God himself, in any conceivable Christian sense, without his own free and loving consent or will. The Catholic Church is compared to an organism, but the metaphor of an organism may be easily misunderstood. Members of our body form a unity but they are not faced with the problem

[2] Moehler: "The Unity of the Church rests finally on the unity of God's own life, which is given us in Jesus Christ by the Spirit of God."

of resolving the problem of their unity or finding an agreement amongst themselves. In the human body the solution is given to them and imposed upon them. But the Christian not only has to ask himself how the problem of unity is resolved in the church; he has further to ask himself how he shall resolve it in his own life.

Hence unity appears to the Christian not simply as a note distinguishing the Church Catholic from all existing religious bodies, but it appears also as an individual problem, as a problem to be solved by each individual each day of his life and in his life as a whole, so that at the Last Judgment he must give an account of how he personally has solved the problem of unity in his own life. By his obedience, by his love, by his justice, by all the acts that he performs, he makes known the fact that he does belong to the one, true church. He himself is a member of that mystical body. To put the moral burden even more drastically, the individual in the Catholic Church has to take upon himself the burden of the entire church. Each part of the human body has to experience the burden of all the rest of it. But in a far deeper, far more poignant sense, each member of the mystical body must endure and take upon himself the burden of the whole.

The existence of such a burden may not be apparent to those who enjoy tranquil and sheltered lives. But there may come at any time, especially in the present time, a gripping consciousness of what that burden implies. There is a vast difference in our realization of such a truth. You may be notionally aware that you are one with a church which contains all races, which regards as equal all nations and racial groups throughout the world. You may realize this simply as something contained in mission magazines, something to be read of and piously meditated upon. It is quite a different thing, however, to experience this world-bond in actual life, to find that one must learn to love and like to get along with those who are of different nationalities and different peoples right in one's own neighborhood: to endure and activate the mystical body in your own city block or neighboring pew in church. My own personal experience shows that many an objection raised against the Catholic Church in practice is caused by the burden imposed by enduring and living with and working with those of such extreme diversity. How often have I heard from those who are not of my faith: they admire our faith, think it beautiful, think it sublime, but they could not endure that intimate association, that intimate bond with people of other political views, other economic status, other nationality, other racial groups, that are implied in that unity which is our concept; in other words, they are not ready to resolve in their own souls, in their own personalities, that burden of unity which is imposed upon us. Yet it is this same burden which evokes the very highest flowering of the human personality.

I have spoken of it as a burden, but it may also be spoken of as a creation because each time that burden is realized one is creating, as it were, the unity of the church. I do not wish to be misunderstood. Unity of the church is not something that is created out of a human agency. Unity of the church is created by the penetration of the individual deeper and deeper into that revelation and unity which is already given him. Now the manner of his penetration, the manner of his creation, may differ enormously. One person may penetrate that unity and that mystery by his profound theological knowledge, his penetrating intellect, his power of organization, or his tremendous personal example. Another may seize its reality only by a very simple faith, by an extremely humble life, obscure and little known. Another person may realize it by offering his sufferings for the rest of the world, by silently enduring privation and sorrow, bearing the burden of the human race in his own private, obscure, and unknown life. There are as many ways of performing that work of creation and realization as there are human beings and human circumstances in the entire world. But that is the work of the church, that is the work that goes on through the ages. Such is this vast robe which is being woven by human hands and built up in all the parts of human life.

Thus curiously enough it is not the unity of the church which makes the severest impact upon the Catholic but rather it is the diversity of the church. In the last analysis it is diversity rather than unity which creates the harsh tensions which are the ultimate trial to one's own humility and patience. The expression of church unity in individual lives increases and fructifies human liberties, giving to them their true role, and thus creates Christian individualities in thought and religious action, who are able to stand up against an external pressure precisely because of the interior principle of their conduct which guides them.

VIII

You may ask me, then, how far do Catholics live up to this high ideal? How far do we find them expressing this unity in their own lives? My answer is that they are limited by the ordinary limitations of humankind. We find vast numbers of those who live up to it in essentials, a smaller number of those who live up to it in its greater heights, on its widest implications. We find grave deficiencies from such a realization; we find sublime realizations. We find men and women to whom the implications of the doctrine of unity and diversity are the very staff of their life; who live by it; they are inspired by it. We find others who accept it in a simple way without conflict but without particular concentration of thought or devotion. We find some who are selective; some who will make a bargain with it; some who are unfaithful to it. We find, in short, all forms of human endeavor just as we find all kinds of variety in the various ways in which it is heroically recognized, in which it is beautifully or piously or nobly expressed. In a word, we find the whole gamut of human sanctity and human endeavor, human interest and human indifference and human sin. All those things we discover, but it remains in every case true that the ultimate test of the church's united fellowship is found in its realization by the individual.

Such a view makes the Catholic exacting to himself, but tolerant to those who are not of his faith. It makes him exacting because he cannot diminish or tarnish the loftiness of the ideal to which his faith has called him. He cannot permit a compromise, a diminution, a lessening of the brightness and the integrity of that faith. He cannot allow a substitute, glittering as it may be, attractive as it may be from a humanitarian or a political standpoint, to come in between. Yet, on the other hand, it makes him tolerant because he realizes, though humbly, what is required of himself, how far he himself falls short of all that that great faith requires of him. And, as I said before, he realizes also how much personal worth there is, how much goodness, how much spiritual religious intuition there may be in many of those who are deprived of a share in his own unity, for reasons for which they are personally not to blame. And he cannot help feeling that if his own concept were better known in its full integrity, a certain degree of opposition to that concept would disappear.

In conclusion let me add that the most efficacious attempts that will ever be made toward reconciliation between the different Christian bodies will chiefly occur on the personal rather than on the formally ecclesiastical scale. It is in lowly living, in humble approach to God, in prayer and penance and good works that the foundation may be laid for common understanding. Neither the worth nor the goodness nor the spirituality of all the best men in it adds one jot or tittle to the perfection and holiness of that revelation to which the Catholic adheres. That revelation is complete and entire. Our work is to penetrate it and realize its vast and sublime depths, not to add our structures. But it is the Catholic's belief that as the world grows closer to God, as the world is humbled, as the world is purified, it will come to a deeper knowledge and an eventual understanding of that mystery of unity and diversity which is his own life and which is the expression, the bond, of his own personal relation with the Saviour himself.

Jᴏʜɴ T. McNᴇɪʟʟ

⊹·*3*·⊹

Protestantism

Mᴏsᴛ of those to whom the term "Protestant" is applied accept the name in the spirit in which a man named Jones consents to be so called. His name is one of the things that have happened to him and to his clan. He may be enthusiastically loyal to his kinsmen while not emotionally stirred by the patronymic he shares with them.

Protestantism existed before it was named. The special application of the word "Protestants" to adherents of the Reformation arose from the Protest which some of them signed in a German imperial diet of 1529. By derivation and classical English usage to protest may equally mean to make an affirmation or a denial; and the Protest of Speyer contained both elements. It was a protest against a negative action, the rescinding of the unanimous decision of an earlier diet which had authorized each state government to act for itself in religion "while awaiting the sitting of the (general) council or national assembly" which the emperor had undertaken to bring about. The Protest was accompanied by an appeal on behalf of "all who receive, or shall receive hereafter, the Word of God," to the de-

46

cision of "a free universal assembly of holy Christendom."

The attachment, through this incident, of the name "Protestants" to the supporters of the Reformation, although unwelcome to them, is thus not entirely misleading. The Protesters were advocates of the authority of the Bible as the Word of God, of responsibility to conscience, and of free assemblies or councils for the reform and direction of the church. The total historic protestation of the Reformers, negative and affirmative, went far beyond these claims but was in substantial accord with them. Protestantism rejected much besides the papal monarchy that was tolerated or espoused by the pre-Reformation church. But anyone who would understand its otherwise perplexing tenacity and energy in the modern world will need to observe what it affirmed not less closely than what it denied. It brought the Bible into a new perspective and made it a great available resource for the layman's religion. It quickened the sense of communion in congregational worship by the use of prayers, hymns, and psalms in which the common people fully shared. The doctrine of the priesthood of all Christians, as a service to others in spiritual things, and a hallowing of the daily task, had great possibilities for the religious enrichment of personal and community life. Justification by faith involved for Luther liberation from a lifeless routine into a joyous activity of service done to God and man in gratitude and freedom—an experience the rich fruit of which has been exemplified in countless lives. The spiritual enhancement of personality (often miscalled by Protestants and others "individualism") in Reformation religion was combined with a vivid assertion of communion and of the mutuality of community life. Protestantism today can afford to lay aside some of its original negations: it needs to revive most of its original affirmations.

Protestantism, the historical movement as distinct from the name, took its rise in different areas and under different leadership. It was never one movement, but began as a series of nearly contemporary and similar manifestations of fresh religious experience and conviction. In the background of these stirrings of new activity many forecasters, with dread or with desire, beheld visions of impending momentous change—the destruction of the church or its revival. The sixteenth century was a century of revival, vastly more religious than the fifteenth or the seventeenth. Personally the Reformers were men of patent faults, but also of high purposes and genuine piety. Interpretations of the Reformation have varied greatly, partly because many of its interpreters have taken no great pains to examine the sources, and especially to examine them objectively. It is right that Protestantism should be judged by its fruits in the modern world; but with erroneous notions of its original ideas and ideals we may ascribe to it fruits that other growths have borne.

Protestantism contains within it a spirit of critical inquiry, and it has never suffered through lack of criticism either from adherents or from opponents. The latter have criticized its principles, or what they thought to be such: the former have lamented what they alleged to be its lapses from principle. There have been critics who have found in Protestantism only a confusion of discordant ideas. To such minds historical Protestantism exhibits a baffling series of variations expressive of a character so fluid and disorderly as to make impossible any definition of the movement in positive terms. They may go so far as to picture it as the mother of all the sectarianism, sectionalism, social confusion, international anarchy, and other woes of the modern world. This view leaves unexplained the sectarianism, confusion, anarchy, and other woes of the era before Protestantism.

Sectarianism unquestionably we have with us. It is one of the chief occasions of anxiety to thoughtful Protestants today. If we are to be adequately aware of the nature of sectarianism, we shall have to observe it in a larger frame of reference than that of post-Reformation Christianity. The sects of the great non-Christian religions are almost innumerable. One writer, especially familiar with Hinduism, has observed no less than twenty-seven causes, largely of a social character, discernible in the origin of these.[1] Despite great discouragement, a countless multitude of sectarian groups arose in the Middle Ages.

Most Protestants view the teeming brood of sects with embarrassment, and not a few of them labor to promote union of the denominations. They feel, too, that in the proliferation of sects Protestantism is not affirming itself but falling short of its own ideals which can be abundantly documented from the statements of its founders and early interpreters. Sectarianism as such is in general disapproval, even on the part of those who exhibit it by declining to entertain a doubt of the superiority of their own sect. Yet there are some who tend to view the sects and schisms as basically healthy manifestations of spiritual liberty and vitality, fruits of a directness of personal faith and an emancipation from institutional authority which they prize above

[1] A. C. Bouquet, *An Introduction to the Study of Efforts at Christian Reunion* (Cambridge, 1914), Chapter 1.

external unity. It should be observed in this connection that there is no more probability of personal spiritual freedom within a small group than within a large one. In fact there are many denominations that neglect the resources of the Christian tradition, operate on a narrow platform of belief, obey an institutional authority highly restrictive of liberty, and through an exclusive spirit and policy forfeit the values of ecumenical fellowship. When invited to unite with other Christians they protect their peculiarities by condemning a unity that is referred to as "external."

The admonitory treatise of the seventeenth-century Puritan, Jeremiah Burroughs, *The Causes, Evils and Cures of Heart and Church Division*, was published in America by Francis Asbury, and was long a book recommended in the Methodist *Discipline*. Burroughs lists and examines the sins that lead to schism, such as pride, envy, jealousy, whispering, meddling, and the divisive course of those who "because they cannot join in all things will join in nothing." We may still profitably read Burroughs, for we still have with us these causes of schism and of its continuance. But a fuller realization of the effect of religious experience upon mental activity, and a deeper awareness of social forces and psychological drives, ought to help us to a more adequate understanding of the roots of sectarianism and of the difficulties involved in overcoming it.

We ought to recognize the tendency of all serious and personally appropriated religion to stimulate independence of thought. Where religion is authoritatively imparted and intelligence is low, there is a disposition to acquiesce in prevailing trends, and this has been conducive to external unity. Christianity, however, stimulates inquiry and thought. We "try the spirits whether they be of God" and we form schools of thought or belief, or individual thinkers lead away from tradition as currently interpreted. This state of things is entirely normal. So long as we have a vigorous Christianity we shall have variety in its interpretation by those who profess it. The sinfulness and the schism come when we intolerantly condemn the sincere religious thoughts of other men, and in personal, party, or institutional pride excommunicate or shun them. There are, needless to say, incidents in which church censures are necessary, and others in which a church falls into errors and abuses justly intolerable to good Christians. But the story of Christianity is marred by a frequently recurring defect of forbearance, and this has been all too obviously a factor in the disunion of Protestantism.

The social causes of sectarian movements are recognized by sociologists and psychologists. Protestantism tends to division by race and social class; parallel phenomena are observed in other religions and in all eras. Are we, then, to accept this as inevitable and irremediable? From a Christian standpoint the answer must be that we dare not so accept it. To recognize it as an historic fact ought to be exceedingly disquieting to Christians. It carries with it an admission that the spirit of Christian love has been so weak as to be ineffectual, or is by nature ineffectual, as a binding agency between racial and economic groups. Christianity claims for itself more than this. A caste system of Christian communions is a travesty on Christianity itself. We may acknowledge the force of the motives that produce this result; but if our religion fails to check and defeat these motives it is a feeble religion scarcely to be recognized as Christianity.

From the days of the Church Fathers down, many Christians have been too ready to anathematize those with whom they could not in all details agree. Many of the Protestant founders warned sharply against this spirit; but in this their practice did not always fully conform to their principle. On some points of doctrine and discipline they became needlessly controversial. "The strength of men's spirit," says Burroughs aptly, and from observation, "is spent in contentions. . . . Contention is a great snare to a man: he wishes he had never meddled with it. . . ." The abounding energy of Protestantism came to be in considerable degree absorbed in controversy, and the movement thereby partially stultified itself for centuries. A change has now come. In our time it is generally possible for us to differ peaceably over the interpretation of a passage of Scripture, and to argue about matters of worship or of church polity, or to inquire into the gravest doctrines, without any thought of excluding the opponent from fellowship. What hinders fellowship now is as much inertia as prejudice. Yet we have not solved the problem which our past willfullness has laid at our door. We are left with a series of major independent Protestant churches and, especially in America, a prodigious array of minor denominations and sects, forming a total picture of ecclesiastical disorder appalling to behold. Some would say that Protestantism today stands where the British stood at El Alamein or the Russians at Stalingrad. These were doubtful battles with much at stake. Richard Hooker was right when he wrote:

For the preservation of Christianity there is not anything more needful, than that such as are of the Visible Church should have mutual fellowship and society one with another.[2]

II

The effort to unite the Protestant churches began with the Reformation. The earnest men who became leaders of the Reformation had passed through the deep places of the soul, and had reached religious certitude through a personal appropriation of grace revealed in the Word of God. This experience came accompanied and conditioned by a radical criticism of the existing hierarchical church system. They abandoned the system, not therewith abandoning the church but intent upon reforming it. Great communities separated by distance from each other, and under different political governments, quickly followed their leadership, and for these communities new statements of belief and forms of church order were adopted. The remarkable thing is not that these formulae exhibit differences in polity and theology; it is that the differences were so minor as to encourage the hope of a future integration. All Protestants retained the basic notion of one Catholic Christian Church. For many years the Lutheran leaders entertained the possibility of a reunion with their German opponents, hoping that this could be attained through church councils with suitable reformation of the entire church of Germany. On occasions almost countless, Lutheran theologians and princes urged the meeting of "a free general Christian council," or at least of a national council, to bring about this

---

[2] *Of the Laws of Ecclesiastical Polity*, III, 1, 14.

end. As late as 1541 Lutherans engaged in conversations with Roman Catholic theologians with a view to a settlement of religion.

Protestantism never was content with its divided state. The development of the Reformed church of Switzerland was accompanied by efforts to unify Swiss and German Protestantism. Various factors prevented the success of these efforts. They would doubtless have had a more favorable reception from the Lutheran side had it not been for the German desire to obtain unity within the Empire to which the Swiss were aliens. The irenic labors of Martin Bucer, Philip Melanchthon, John Calvin, Theodore Beza, John à Lasco, and other leading figures in sixteenth-century Protestantism; the brotherly kindness and hospitality of Henry Bullinger of Zurich to exiled English Protestants; the benefactions and friendliness of Archbishop Cranmer to exiled or visiting Continental leaders and his plan for a consensus of the Reformation churches, are factors in the history of that period important as evidence of what men desired rather than what they achieved. But such agreements as the Wittenberg Concord of the Oberland and north German churches (1536), the Zurich Consensus of the French-speaking and German-speaking Swiss (1549), the Consensus of Sendomir of Lutherans, Calvinists, and Bohemian Brethren in Poland (1570), and the Confession adopted by Utraquists, Lutherans, Calvinists, and Bohemian Brethren and approved by a Bohemian diet at Prague (1574) stand as evidence of a real concern for unity, and some progress in attaining it, at an early stage in the development of Protestantism. A large measure of theological agreement is shown by the collection of material from the confessions of faith in a book prepared at Geneva and published in 1581, *The Harmony of Orthodox and Reformed Confessions of Faith.*

But such results were wholly inadequate to arrest the process by which Protestantism became divided in course of its expansion. The seventeenth century witnessed a series of fresh efforts to bring the divergent churches into fellowship. Within the Protestant ranks the fundamental schism was between Lutheran and Reformed. Lutherans in a series of nations were in substantial agreement, and the series of Reformed churches also lived in mutual reciprocity. So long as religious scholars still used Latin that language was a means of intercourse; but by the end of the seventeenth century few Protestant theological works appeared in Latin, and no international language of scholarship for Europe was in general use. The publication of opinion-forming books almost exclusively in one or another of the competing national languages has been one of the prime factors in the intellectual disintegration of Europe. It affected the churches, weakening the links that bound them in international fellowship.

The seventeenth century witnessed numerous brave efforts to create or restore the bonds of union. Professor Batten's careful study of the career of John Dury,[3] while concentrating attention on one apostle of unity, sheds light on the views and aims of many of its other advocates in that age. The heroic and pathetic failure of Dury, the ill-success of Calixtus, the futility of the proposals of Comenius, Usher, Stillingfleet, the "Aberdeen Doctors," Baxter, Leib-

[3] J. M. Batten, *John Dury, Advocate of Christian Reunion* (Chicago: University of Chicago Press, 1944).

niz, and innumerable other seekers of Catholic unity in Protestantism are material well worthy of careful study and sober reflection. The prevalence of narrow if sincere convictions, bigotry, and inertia in the churches, and the effect of many adverse political interests are factors in the situation. No popular passion for reunion was aroused by the theological leaders, and the movements they sponsored remained largely in the area of elementary negotiation and learned discussion.

The eighteenth century saw the resumption of similar efforts and proposals, but with less zeal and no better success. The church policies of the enlightened despots did not encourage international churchmanship or spontaneous church movements of any kind. Sectarians were not conciliated, but rendered so uncomfortable that many of them sought escape to the New World. In England Nonconformity took its modern denominational forms. A movement so tolerant and catholic in spirit as Wesleyanism was led, or obliged, to form a separate church. In Scotland pressure of the state upon the national church led to a series of secessions which were to culminate in the Disruption of 1843. The effect of all this upon the church situation in America, at the time of the founding of the Republic and thereafter, was to bring Lutheran and Reformed elements and a variety of sects from the Continent to mingle in this country with Anglicans, English Nonconformists of numerous varieties, and Scottish and Irish Seceders, thus rendering the hope of unification remote indeed. As has been vividly indicated by Dean Sperry in Chapter 1, the American religious scene has since become still more confused.

Shall we ever emerge from this confusion? More Protestants than ever are impatiently asking this question.

III

The past century has seen the gradual upgrowth of a cumulative movement toward unity in Protestantism, looking ultimately toward the complete unification of Christianity. The movement has a very long way to go and many grave obstacles to overcome; but it is undoubtedly going forward with prayer and purpose and enlisting the approval, even the zealous support, of many church members to a degree unprecedented in the history of similar efforts. The movement has been largely a phenomenon of the English-speaking churches, but it has derived great stimulation from fresh currents in Continental theology as well as from the service of able leaders of the Swedish, Swiss, German, and French churches. Since it is participated in by Eastern Orthodox and Old Catholics as well as Anglicans, it is more than Protestant in its range.

The Ecumenical Movement is twofold. It embraces the processes of local interdenominational negotiations for union, and the effort to bring into progressively richer fellowship the churches of every people of the world.

Historians will have difficulty in marking the point of its origin. Its rise can be explained only when it is recognized that all the participating churches have always believed in the natural ecumenicity of Christianity, and in varying measure have desired to see this realized. It represents no new principle, but the fresh recognition of one that is constant, though in the past often scandalously obscured. The

revival of missionary activity that began in the last decade
of the eighteenth century as a product of the Evangelical
Revival established outposts of Christianity in many lands.
In time the expansion of these laid upon the home
churches problems of adjustment and comity that de-
manded interdenominational and often international coöperation, while they strongly suggested the desirability of
fuller unity. When certain groups of Presbyterian seceders
ended their controversies by reunion in Canada, Ireland,
and Scotland (1817-1820) a process was instituted that has
gradually enlarged to effect unions of many substantial
churches. In addition, the new technology of transportation
and communication set up an unprecedented global activity, and made possible a new intimacy of the peoples, and
of the Christians, dwelling in all parts of the world. In our
own century even the newer American sects tend to propa-
gate themselves in farthest Asia, and native sons of India
and China have been figures of distinction in ecumenical
conferences. These three elements, then—the new evangelical world-mission, the craving for a wider fellowship, and
the enhanced opportunity of international intercourse—go
far to explain how the movement for ecumenical unity became a modern possibility.

The formation of the Evangelical Alliance (1845-46)
and its subsequent cultivation of an evangelical and theo-
logically cautious internationalism should be recognized as
a contributing element. The Alliance revived the seventeenth-century motto, "In things necessary, unity; in things
indifferent, liberty; in all things, charity." It was probably
the most important agency of the late nineteenth century in
creating a sense of common interest among the numerous

branches of Protestantism. Comparable with it, and probably of greater importance for ecumenical Christianity, was the series of meetings of bishops of the Anglican communion at Lambeth Palace which began in 1867. It was at the third Lambeth Conference in 1888 that the formula known as the Lambeth Quadrilateral was adopted.[4] This simplified basis of church unity in its final clause referred to "the Historic Episcopate, locally adapted in the methods of its administration. . . ." This brought at once into the foreground of discussion the doctrine of the ministry and the problem of the variant polities of the churches. The utterances of later Lambeth Conferences, especially that of 1920, have deeply affected the course of union discussion and drawn forth fresh interest in the problems of unity. The good relations of Anglicanism with other episcopally governed churches, especially those of the Eastern Orthodox family, along with the friendliness of some of its ablest leaders for nonepiscopal churches, have given it a key position in ecumenical projects. Whatever action the churches of the Anglican fellowship may take or decline to take, their decisions are sure to determine in some degree how far and how fast the movement may go. The variety of attitudes within Anglicanism toward those without dictates what may seem an ingloriously dilatory policy on the part of the leaders. A Roman Catholic satirist half a century ago treated amusingly the union proposals then talked of in England.[5] A grand council is held in which all groups are

[4] With slight alterations it was taken over from the "Quadrilateral of pure Anglicanism" set forth in 1870 in an American book, *The Church Idea*, by W. R. Huntington. It had already in 1886 been endorsed by a Chicago meeting of the Protestant Episcopal General Convention.

[5] A. F. Marshall, *The Comedy of English Protestantism* (1896).

represented. The whole is a picture of futility. A Wesleyan offers to enter the Church of England tomorrow if he can be shown what the Church of England is. He finally concludes that it does not exist. With us its existence is not, of course, in question: no church appears to have a firmer hold on existence. But a great church must be broad enough to include many narrow people, and this is its embarrassment. An English Methodist recently complained that "to many Anglicans the Exarch of Bulgaria is more important than the Moderator of the Free Church Assembly." [6] There are doubtless many others of whom the reverse statement would be true. One hundred years from now possibly no voice will be raised in blame of an Englishman for having an immoderate affection for the Exarch of Bulgaria, who assuredly needs all the Christian friends he can get. Dr. Harrison is understandably impatient with the Anglicans for lamenting "our unhappy divisions" and doing so little about them. But the Anglican communion has long passed the stage of indifference. After the First World War, the Lambeth Conference, in an impressive message on Christian unity, affirmed the principle of "mutual deference to one another's consciences," and held the ministries of the Free Churches to be "real ministries of Christ's word and Sacraments." Yet every move to implement these statements in action is viewed with alarm by high church elements, and meets with hindrances from them. Most Anglicans hold with Hooker that the nonepiscopal ministries even if "real" are "defective." The question that arises today in the minds of many Protestants is whether after the present war Angli-

[6] A. W. Harrison, *The Evangelical Revival and Christian Reunion* (1942), p. 188.

canism, including its American, Canadian, Australian, and other branches, will go forward in the spirit of 1920 or postpone commitments to Protestantism as a whole and so, for a time at least, surrender its preëminence in the movement for a world-wide church.

IV

The Ecumenical Movement has its roots in the past, but its chief growth has taken place in the twentieth century. The Edinburgh Missionary Conference of 1910 far outclassed in importance the preceding world conferences on missions that had been held occasionally for over half a century. The continuation committee set up at Edinburgh (later becoming the International Missionary Council), made arrangements for other world meetings, including those held at Jerusalem in 1928 and at Madras in 1938. Both these conferences, largely attended by leaders of the indigenous Christian communities, adopted strong statements in favor of organic union. Another stream of development came with the conferences on Faith and Order, a movement begun in 1910 on the initiative of Bishop Charles H. Brent, which held an important exploratory conference at Lausanne in 1927. Its great gathering at Edinburgh in 1937 was timed to follow immediately the Life and Work Conference held at Oxford. Archbishop Nathan Söderblom of Uppsala fathered the Life and Work movement, which, with the coöperation of the Evangelical Alliance, the Federal Council of Churches, and the Patriarch of Constantinople, held a notable world meeting at Stockholm in 1925. Representative leaders of many churches from many lands were becoming accustomed to discussion together of the common problems of the Christian cause and of the means of effective permanent coöperation. In 1937 world affairs were menacing. The delegates at Oxford and Edinburgh conferred under the shadow of impending war, and set forth valuable statements that will undoubtedly be reverted to for a long time to come. But their most important act was their joint creation of a plan for a World Council of Churches. This has since been partially organized and has obtained the adherence of eighty-five churches including all the larger communions except the Roman Catholic, and with adherents numbering about 350 millions. Despite discouraging losses by death of several leaders of this organization, there is little reason to doubt that it will become increasingly influential as an agency for the coördination of Christian action, for the encouragement of federal and, where possible, corporate unity everywhere. Regional ecumenical conferences have been possible during the war. One was held in Toronto, for North America, in 1941, and in 1942 representatives of churches of the Axis-dominated countries and Sweden met at Sondershausen, Germany. The World Council itself is still "in process of formation," and may take some time to pass this stage. The structure of organization will in all probability embrace local, national, and regional councils subordinate to the World Council, and general assemblies to be held at intervals of some years. Existing world organizations of denominations may be represented in the Council.

Most denominations have for some time been cultivating their own international unity. Shortly after the first of the Lambeth Conferences there was formed the Alliance of Reformed Churches Holding the Presbyterian System (1875), and it was soon followed by the Ecumenical Methodist Conference (1881) and later by the International Congregational Council (1891), the Baptist World Alliance (1905), the Lutheran World Convention (1923), and the Association for Liberal Christianity. The last named of these calls for special comment in this context. The Unitarian, Universalist, and other churches designated Liberal, are at present in an ambiguous position in relation to the World Council. A number of the Liberal churches, keenly interested in the social expression of Christianity, were active participants in the Life and Work movement. But the preliminary formula of the World Council employs a phrase taken over from the Faith and Order movement that evidently excludes them from membership: "churches that accept Jesus Christ as their God and Saviour." The late Dr. William Adams Brown pointed out that this language is objectionable from a conservative as well as from a liberal viewpoint. It is not unlikely that the terms of membership will be revised in the permanent plan of the Council; but to reach a formula inclusive enough to give opportunity of membership both to the Liberal group of churches and to those who stand on guard for the traditional trinitarianism is a task sure to present no little difficulty. The work of the International Council of Religious Liberals, founded in 1900 and normally holding triennial world meetings since 1901, has been continued since 1930 by the Association for Liberal Christianity and Religious Freedom. This association coördinates the world-wide activities of the member churches, which have been firmly organized in about ten countries of Continental Europe, in most parts of the English-speaking world, and in India, Japan, Palestine, and the Philippine Islands.

The Federal Council of Churches of Christ in America since its organization in the period 1905-1908 has rendered increasingly valuable service toward Protestant coöperation. The Federal Council of Evangelical Free Churches in England had its beginning in 1917 and was reorganized in 1940 as the Free Church Council. It has been in extended negotiations with the Church of England. In 1942 the British Council of Churches was formed. It has been active in efforts to bring a religious message to the common man, and in laying plans for educational advance, and for the restoration of ecclesiastical buildings destroyed and damaged in the war. Since 1925 Scotland has had its own Scottish Churches Council which is not a federation of churches but a mechanism for consultation among church leaders. Ireland has its United Council of Christian Churches. The Canadian Council of Churches was formed in 1944. In Australia—where negotiations for a Congregational, Methodist, and Presbyterian union were renewed in 1938—plans for a federation of Protestant churches are well advanced. An active federation is at work in New Zealand. The Christian Council of South Africa takes a practical interest in that country's social and racial problems. Everywhere great projects are entertained and efforts made in common by numerous churches working through representative councils.

Meanwhile a great many denominations have been engaged in union negotiations and in a considerable number of cases combinations have been effected, usually at the cost of much labor and protracted discussion. A mere list of these achievements and projects would occupy many pages. Dr. H. Paul Douglass, examining the negotiations and consummations of union in the decade 1927-1936, observed an increasing bulk of effort toward union. The evidence he has presented for the six years 1937-1942 appears to show a continuation of this trend. The present war has increased the desire of Christians for fellowship with other Christians, and there is no reason to expect a return to the old denominational spirit. But the processes of union are slow. The inertia of great bodies highly organized; the investment of funds, and still more of emotion and responsibility, in existing worthy denominational enterprises which union would disturb; the interests of salaried and influential personnel; the task of persuading the unwilling; the labor of finding acceptable phrases for the documents of agreement; the researches in denominational and general church history involved in discussion of the issues; and the complicated problems of church property and trusts—these are some of the factors that make the attainment of any union costly in time and patience. Bishop Francis J. McConnell has noted that "in one form or another the task of Methodist reunion ran through sixty years." This union, completed in 1939, ended one of the unhappy separations incidental to the slavery issue and created the largest Protestant church in the United States. In Canada denominational reunions had come about in the nineteenth century. After long negotiations and repeated delays the United Church of Canada was formed in 1925 of the Congregational, Methodist, and Presbyterian churches, some Presbyterians dissenting. The Presbyterian churches of Scotland, save for very small minorities, were united in 1929, and the major segments of British Methodism in 1932. The two French Reformed churches, severed in 1874, were reunited in 1939. In North and South India projects for uniting a variety of denominations have been in negotiation for decades: in both areas favorable action appears ultimately probable. The South India proposals are for the union of Anglican with presbyterially governed churches, and involve the mutual recognition of orders and ultimately ordination by bishops. A factor of notable significance in India is the indigenous mission effort of the National Missionary Society of India founded in 1905, one of whose purposes is "to promote unity among Christians." Presbyterian and Anglican churches in Iran are also considering a plan of union. The Church of Christ in China arose between 1918 and 1927, gathering into a rather free union a number of Protestant mission churches. In Japan and occupied China the government has favored and hastened Protestant unions as a part of national policy. In Germany the Nazi plan to coördinate the churches (1933) proved highly objectionable and met with failure.

In the United States at present many denominations are engaged in active conversations and negotiations looking toward union. These efforts are in fact so prevalent that they involve a large proportion of the churches holding membership in the Federal Council. Some of them are negotiating with more than one sister denomination. The Presbyterian Church in the U. S. A. is about equally engaged with the Presbyterian Church in the U. S. and with the Protestant Episcopal Church. The Protestant Episcopal General Convention of 1937 invited the Presbyterians to follow it in declaring their "purpose to achieve organic unity." The possibility of success in either or both of these efforts cannot be dismissed, though no prompt conclusion of either union is to be expected. The Southern Presbyterians are also in negotiations with three smaller Presbyterian churches. The branches of Lutheranism in America have been approaching one another with a view to ultimate union, and a unification of the United Lutheran and American Lutheran churches is apparently in prospect. A program of close coöperation has recently been adopted by Canadian Lutheran groups. The Missouri Synod in both the United States and Canada, however, has been disinclined to unite with others. The Congregational Christian Churches, formed in 1931 of the denominations indicated in the double name, and the Evangelical and Reformed Church, formed by a comparable union in 1934, have now negotiated an agreement to unite which awaits final action in 1947. If this plan materializes, within about fifteen years four denominations will have become one. New and strange sects and cults continue to appear, but the number of union projects in active negotiation or discussion may be regarded as more than an offset to these divisive groups. If all the projected unions should be favorably concluded, a substantial reduction in the number of denominations would result. Even if half of them succeed within a reasonably short time, the change will be impressive.

v

Among the older branches of Protestantism the pursuit of unity has never been so purposeful as it is today. Much more than formerly, the pulpit and the denominational press reflect the rising interest in unity and in the progress of world Christianity, and keep the people aware of it. The radio is beginning to play a part in spreading the revival. The churches, to a degree not hitherto shown, are astir with a desire to coöperate and to combine, and are intent upon building a universal permanent federation by which Christian communion and coöperation will be promoted. It is not meant by this that all Protestants share the new enthusiasm, or that it is the dominant concern of many. Indifference is widespread, and serious resistance can be found. What is meant is that the interest is great enough to produce action leading by slow steps in the definite direction of the widest possible unification.

The question may arise whether this trend is due to denominational weariness and discouragement rather than to a genuine zeal for an ecumenical expression of Christianity. Some of the denominations concerned have not been prosperous. In the years of economic depression church budgets shrank. The business mind is dissatisfied with wasteful overlapping. Union may be approved by some as an economic measure. The pressure of irreligious forces and the feebleness of a separate testimony may have reduced denominational self-esteem. United we may stand though divided we should fall. Are we uniting because we are beaten? The rising flood of religiously illiterate new sects on the one hand, and the rising strength of Roman Catholicism with its example of solid unity on the other, may be forcing us unwillingly to clasp each other's hands.

Consideration should be given to all these as possible partial explanations of the ecumenical revival of Protestantism. But it is hardly possible that any or all of these elements constitute the full explanation. The movement appears to press forward with unhurried pace and steady momentum, and with a resourcefulness of mind and spirit not born of escapism and fear. Groups of theological scholars diligently labor to draw up memoranda for its guidance in solving difficulties in polity and doctrine and for the clarification of social and ethical problems confronting the churches. The straightforward approach to the stupendous problems of the war and social rehabilitation by ecumenical leaders and groups suggests rather that we have begun to respond with new vigor to the world's need. May it not be, then, that in this revival Protestantism is at last coming to itself? Believing in ecumenicity, it has heretofore in large degree practiced segregation. Believing in the fullest use of conferences and councils as a means of spiritual enrichment, reform, and government of the church, it has too largely confined these to narrow limits. Believing in a church visible extended through the world, it has operated on a national or regional basis, with only denominational missions to extend it into some of the regions beyond. The early Protestants repeatedly called for "a free general Christian council." They used the conciliar principle for their small denominational affairs, but global and ecumenical conciliarism was an expectation indefinitely postponed. Now the churches are breaking the bonds of old denominational habit and together taking the world for their parish. Perhaps we can republish with some sense of reality the words of Schleiermacher: *Die Reformation geht noch fort* —Protestantism goes marching on. It goes, however, in intimate company with communions not strictly Protestant, and ventures to hope for a continual approach to complete Christian unity.

Dr. Ross Sanderson, in a helpful study of "The Philosophy of Church Coöperation," has these sentences:

Once again conciliar Christianity faces a great historic opportunity, this time with far larger hope of success [than in the fifteenth century] by reason of the gains achieved during four Protestant centuries. . . . *We move toward a time when the entire church will function ecumenically at all levels,* through the coöperative churchmanship of all communions.[7]

The after-war era, in religious as in other matters, defies prediction. We begin to see only some of the alternative possibilities. For the faiths discussed in this book there will in all probability be decades of extraordinary opportunity. There will be immeasurable sorrows to be healed, bitter hatreds to be overcome, lost pathways to be found again, and new direction to be given to bewildered and misguided youth. Organized religion will have to undertake greater services than ever before: otherwise it will fail miserably to bring spiritual deliverance, hope, purpose, and dignity to men. At best the prospect is not bright for the near future. But religious men have no reason to despair. If a real peace and a true freedom are established and if adequate channels of peaceful world intercourse are developed, the reconciling influence of religion and its power to redirect men's attitudes may in time provide correctives for the major evils and perils that confront us. Through the ecumenical revival, which has developed steadily in this distraught century, the Protestant and associated churches may hope to find themselves in a position to yield their share of service more effectively than ever before.

[7] *Christendom,* IX (1944), 490. (The italics are the author's.)

4

Judaism

ABOUT one hundred generations have passed since Moses, harking back to the faith of his ancestors, initiated the process which has led to the emergence not only of Rabbinic Judaism, but also of Christianity and Islam. It is of the essence of Judaism to regard this whole period as one of continuing preparation for a Messianic Age, when men will serve God with far greater devotion and singleness of purpose than has yet been evinced among them. All the monotheistic religions have a share, according to Maimonides, in preparing the way for the coming of this age; it is natural that a Jew should believe that his particular contribution is indispensable as well as unique. To the Jew, therefore, Judaism is neither an archaeological anachronism nor a social problem. On the contrary, it is a living force in world civilization and a vital element in the solution of the intricate and perplexing general problem of human life.

To make his contribution to the emergence of an age of better men and a better world, the Jew, if he accepts his traditions, will have to organize his life with the care usually reserved in other faiths for members of religious

71

orders. The great codes of rabbinic law, those of Maimonides and of Joseph Caro, are meticulous, almost pedantic, in their regulations of the Jew's daily life. In the hands of the expert in rabbinic law it becomes a pageant, with stage directions at every step. Washing on awakening is not a matter of choice, hygiene, pleasure, or good manners; it is a commandment. One must pay respect to one's body by keeping it clean, because it is a reflection of God's divinity. Dressing properly is again not submission to fashion, but part of one's duty as a child of God to oneself and to one's fellow men. Before eating one must recite the daily prayers. At breakfast one is, from the point of view of Judaism, participating in an act of worship. It is, therefore, necessary to wash the hands anew, as did the priests when about to offer sacrifice in the Temple, and to recite a blessing before and after eating. Particularly meticulous Jews will each day make a gift for a charitable purpose before offering their morning prayer, to fulfill the verse, "and thy righteousness shall go before thee." They will set aside some time, either before their morning meal or immediately after it, for the study of the law; so that each day will be the occasion of the threefold worship of God—prayer, kindness to the suffering, and study.

Such regulations cover the whole day's interests and affairs. If, after a lapse of thirty days, one sees for the first time a particularly close friend, that is an occasion for a blessing to God. A new fruit, marking the beginning of a season for that particular product, calls for an expression of gratitude. On the receipt of bad news one must recite a prayer accepting God's judgment as righteous.

These matters may strike the outsider as exotic. But

to the initiate they are as serious as, for example, the right word to the man of letters, or the correct note to the musician. When the pageant moves from the realm of ritual, which tends to be arbitrary (and which our materialistic civilization finds it hard to appreciate), to that of ethics, the importance of such actions becomes clear. If walking in the street the Jew sees an old man or a cripple ahead, he is expected to slacken his pace, lest he recall the infirm to a sense of deprivation. If a rabbinic student finds himself in a situation of conflicting rights in which the issues are not clear, he must yield, lest by insisting on his special prerogatives he bring the whole Talmudic tradition and with it the Name of God into disrepute. This would be the sin of Hillul Ha-Shem (profaning the Name of God) with regard to which the unwitting are as guilty as the witting. In conversation he must watch his speech not only against derogation of his neighbor, but also against excessive praise, for undue praise is likely to evoke dispraise, and so he would lead his neighbor into the sin of defamation. When he goes home, he must avoid any harsh word for his wife, "for the oppression of woman is a graver sin than the oppression of man; the tears of women come easier, and therefore the sin of oppressing them is the more to be avoided." If tyrannical in his home, a man may frighten the members of his family into concealing their derelictions from him, and drive them to falsehoods.

The rules covering daily life, in all its aspects, are so many and varied that to list them would require a volume many times the size of this. Obviously, few Jews of the present day observe them in every way. Some indeed are quite oblivious of them and try to build their lives through a personal application of the general principles of ethics to each new situation.

Jewish tradition holds these Jews, though perhaps utterly unobservant, as within the fold. They are the group whom Judaism regards as subject to its rules, whether or not they agree. The principle of the Jewish tradition is that the child of Jewish parents (or, in the case of a mixed relationship, of a Jewish mother) is a Jew. He is bound by the covenant into which Moses entered for the children of Israel and their descendants. This covenant was reaffirmed by Ezra; and has been accepted by all the proselytes; so that the descendants of proselytes also are Jews.

In this sense, therefore, Judaism is a "kinship" group. But there is no "Jewish race." The great spiritual centers of Judaism, and with them the centers of Jewish population, have moved from region to region, and even from continent to continent, during the past twenty centuries; and these movements of the great centers of learning and inspiration have helped accentuate the social process by which all western groups have become biologically intermingled. So complete has been the admixture of peoples since the days of Moses, and particularly since the destruction of the Second Jewish Commonwealth, that today the Jew of western Europe is as different from the Jew of south Arabia as is the Christian of western Europe from the Moslem of south Arabia.

These divisions among the Jews, according to their lands and their family backgrounds, are reinforced by differences of ritual. The two great groups of Jews in the western world are those of Ashkenazic or north European descent, and the Sephardic or those of Spanish-Portuguese descent. The two have maintained different rituals throughout the generations, pray in different kinds of synagogues, and differ widely in their forms.

Toward the end of the eighteenth century there arose a group in Polish Jewry which revolted against the excessive emphasis on intellectualism in the Talmudic Judaism of their day. They insisted that the main emphasis in Judaism should be on simple piety, rather than on the study of the Talmud. This group, whose views and philosophy came to be differently interpreted among different types of followers, became known as the Hasidim (pietists). (This eighteenth-century European group must be distinguished from a group by the same name, which arose two thousand years earlier in Palestine, and which is mentioned in the Book of the Maccabees, as well as in rabbinic literature.) There are still many adherents of this group, perhaps a million. Their opponents were known as Mitnagdim (literally, opponents). The difference between these two groups is less important in America than it was in Europe, and is rapidly fading. But at the beginning of the century the synagogues of the two types of Ashkenazic Jews were quite distinct, and in some localities there was even considerable animosity between them.

There are other rites which differ more widely from both the Ashkenazic and Sephardic than these do from each other. Of these rites, the most important are those of the Yemenite Jews of south Arabia now emigrating very rapidly into Palestine; of the Persian Jews; of the Jews of north Africa; and of certain isolated groups in India.

II

There are also many Jews whose association with the main stream of Jewish tradition is rather tenuous. Of these the most famous are the Falashas, the group descended from Abyssinians converted to Judaism in ancient times, who have retained the Jewish tradition in a peculiar form until this day. They regard themselves as Jews, though their customs and manner differ widely from that of the Rabbinic Jews. Many Falashas are now associating themselves with formal, traditional Judaism. There once was a group of Chinese Jews, who had reached China in early Christian centuries by way of Persia, and had become assimilated to the environment in every respect except religion. During the course of the nineteenth century the last remnants of this community disappeared and it is now recalled only as a historical curiosity. In the Near East there are said to be at present about twenty-five thousand Jews, who are compelled by their neighbors outwardly to conform to the Moslem faith, but secretly preserve their Jewish tradition. In Portugal groups still survive whose ancestors were Jews forcibly converted to Christianity. They tried to retain in secret such Jewish life as they could; and their descendants to this day observe some of the Jewish rituals, and know that they are not Christians. The historian and sociologist note that these descendants of the Jews of the fifteenth century now think some of the customs forced upon them by the need of secrecy are authentic Jewish customs; and that those who have not had to resort to these devices are violating the law. Thus they believe that synagogues must be placed underground, where they will be hidden from dangerous eyes. These secret Jews are called Marranos.

There are said to be in Mexico about three thousand Jews descended from Indians converted to Judaism, and from mixed marriages between Indians and Marranos. They practice their faith openly today, and regard themselves as Jews.

In Harlem in the City of New York, and perhaps elsewhere in the United States, there are some Negro Jews. Most of these are probably descended from Negro slaves of Jewish owners in the West Indies. Just as the slaves of Christians tended to become Christian, so the slaves of Jews became Jews. Their descendants, now free, practice a variation of the Jewish faith.

These small groups on the fringe of Jewish life, as it were, do not of course affect the development of the main stream of Judaism. This has been preserved among the Jews who have retained the Hebrew language as that of prayer and worship, whose rabbis, at least, studied and knew the Talmud, observed the basic Talmudic precepts in all their lives, and considered conformity in all the details of Talmudic law an ideal.

The transformation of life in western Europe as a result of the Industrial Revolution has brought about a development which cuts across the distinctions of tradition among these Jews—namely, the rise of new approaches to Judaism, unknown to past generations. Of these the oldest is Reform or Liberal Judaism. Its basic characteristic is its break with normative tradition, which regards Judaism as a system of revealed law. The Reform Jews claim the authority to alter the law, even in such basic matters as the manner of observing the Sabbath, or the appropriate forms to be followed in marriage and divorce. The synagogue ritual of Reform Jews differs basically from that found in any of the older rites. It contains a large admixture of the vernacular; in some types of Reform all references to the return to Palestine are omitted together with references to the Resurrection of the Dead.

In America the rabbis who adhere to Reform Judaism have organized themselves as the Central Conference of American Rabbis. The congregations to which they minister form the Union of American Hebrew Congregations. The seminaries which train rabbis for these congregations, and are largely under their influence, are the Hebrew Union College in Cincinnati and the Jewish Institute of Religion in New York. The latter, while adopting Reform standards for the worship in its synagogue and accepting them for the life of its faculty and students, claims that it trains students for the rabbinate irrespective of denominationalism within Judaism.

The establishment of Reform Judaism in America as an effective movement persuaded some of the Conservative rabbis of the time of the need of establishing an American seminary to train rabbis for traditional congregations. There thus emerged in the year 1886 the Jewish Theological Seminary of America, which has become the fountainhead for what is generally known as Conservative (or historical) Judaism in this country. The rabbis graduated from this Seminary, and others whom they have admitted to their ranks, have organized themselves as the Rabbinical Assembly of America; and their congregations are organized in the United Synagogue of America. Conservative Judaism has not yet formulated any definite platform, distinguishing it as a denomination within Judaism. Indeed, many of its leaders deny that such a platform can be formulated; for they hold that it is of the essence of the Conservative Jewish movement to regard Judaism as an evolving faith, which must tolerate and even encourage wide differences. While preaching maximal observance of Jewish law, these leaders refuse to read out of the Jewish fold men who fail to follow these observances. There is a unifying pattern of life among the men who are trained at the Seminary, by virtue of their common background; but these leaders refuse to agree to any reduction of this pattern of life to a codified statement, holding that this would create a new denomination within Judaism, whereas Conservative Judaism seeks to avoid denominationalism as such.

Many other members and leaders of the Conservative Jewish movement regard it as a denomination which, yielding to conditions of our time on certain details of the law, still seeks to maintain respect for basic Jewish tradition. They regard it as impractical and even contrary to fact to maintain that Conservative Judaism is not a denomination in the sense that Reform Judaism is; they believe that the very complicated approach to Conservative Judaism described above, maintaining on the one hand an association of congregations and rabbis with common ideals and a common pattern of life, and on the other hand denying that this association constitutes a wing within Judaism, will end in the frustration of the whole movement. The argument between these two groups in Conservative Judaism is at present (1945) at its height.

One result which may be attributed to the refusal of

leading Conservative Jews to formulate a program for their group has been the rise of Reconstructionism. This movement revolves about the conception of Judaism as a religious civilization, a conception which, more than any other, stresses the cultural and communal aspects in addition to the religious aspects of Jewish life. While it originated among Conservative Jews, Reconstructionism now includes many who are Reform, and some who are Orthodox. Their dominant philosophy is a belief in Jewish tradition, but that this tradition must be reinterpreted and when necessary even amended to meet the problems of modern life.

A large group of rabbis and congregations have taken the attitude that the tolerance of Conservative Jews for deviation from tradition, itself constitutes a deviation; and that the whole emphasis on the historical development of Judaism, characteristic of Conservative Jewish congregations and rabbis, is a rejection of basic principles of Judaism. The groups taking this attitude are usually described as Orthodox Jews. In America there are at present a number of rabbinical seminaries training rabbis for Orthodox congregations. Of these the largest and oldest is the Rabbi Isaac Elhanan Theological Seminary, also known as the Yeshiva. (This institution is unique among rabbinic schools in that it maintains, in addition to its theological faculty, a school of liberal arts.) The other schools taking the same general attitude are: The Hebrew Theological College in Chicago, the Mesifta Torah Va-Daat in Brooklyn, and the Mesifta Rabbi Hayyim Berlin, also in Brooklyn. The rabbis who hold this general view are organized in the Union of Orthodox Rabbis (Agudat Ha-Rabbonim), the Histadrut Ha-Rabbonim, and other smaller and less well-known groups. There is only one congregational organization of this group, the Union of Orthodox Jewish Congregations of America, which includes only a small number of the congregations which share the Orthodox point of view.

III

Within recent years the various religious groups have united to establish The Synagogue Council of America, which thus claims authority to speak for the religious Jews of the country. Its effectiveness has been considerably hampered by the fact that by its constitution it requires unanimous consent of all constituent bodies for any major decision; that its administration changes every two years; and by its lack of any suitable means to carry out its projects. It is at present problematical whether the difficulties which Jews now face in maintaining their faith, and the need for common action, will help strengthen the Council. One of its problems arises from the fact that at least one major group, the Union of Orthodox Rabbis and their congregations, have failed to associate themselves with it. This is because the Union, consisting largely of rabbis trained in the traditional Jewish academies abroad, does not regard the graduates of American seminaries generally as having rabbinic authority, and therefore cannot associate itself with an institution in which their rabbinic authority is accepted and thus tacitly approved.

Without taking sides in these purely religious differences and yet deeply affecting them, as well as all other aspects of Jewish life, there has within the past fifty years arisen a new movement which is beginning to direct Jewish thought into new channels and is raising entirely new issues. This is the school of thought and action centering about the program of political Zionism. The concept that the place of Palestine in Judaism is unique and preëminent is, of course, not limited to political Zionists. Virtually all Jews, except some small groups among the Reform Jews and the unaffiliated, accept this principle. From time immemorial Jewish tradition has looked upon the Holy Land as the focus of the Jewish faith; in prayer all Jews throughout the generations have turned their faces toward Palestine and Jerusalem; the restoration of a predominant Jewish settlement there has been a center of Jewish aspiration for sixty generations since the time of Vespasian and Titus. The issues which have arisen about political Zionism concern the character which this restored settlement should have, and the rights which should be sought for it. As formulated under the guidance of Theodore Herzl, Zionism seeks "a publicly recognized, legally secure" home for the Jewish people in Palestine. This Basle program has crystallized in the Balfour Declaration, in which Great Britain, on November 2, 1917, assured the Jewish people that "His Majesty's Government view with favour the establishment in Palestine of a national home for the Jewish people, and will use their best endeavors to facilitate the achievement of this object. . . ." The Balfour Declaration has since been incorporated into the mandate for Palestine given to Great Britain at the San Remo Conference of 1920.

There are some Jews both among the observant and the nonobservant who do not accept this development. Among these may be counted the members of Agudath Israel, an Orthodox Jewish organization which, accepting the central place of Palestine in Judaism, objects to the fact that Zionism includes among its adherents many who reject traditional Jewish belief and practice, and that many Zionist institutions are not being developed in conformity with the Jewish religion. Among the Zionists themselves, there is the group of the Mizrachi, who are Orthodox Jews, but regard it as appropriate to work with other Zionists for the common cause. There are also Poale Zion (workers of Zion) who are socialist Zionists, and other leftist groups in the World Zionist Organization.

A group of political Zionists, who have found that the policies pursued by the World Zionist Organization were not sufficiently effective, have organized themselves as the New Zionist Organization. They are usually known as "Revisionists" and they insist on the immediate establishment and recognition of Palestine, including Transjordan, as a Jewish State.

The platform of political Zionism has led to the emergence of a number of other groups and committees, taking various attitudes with regard to the main issue. Some are even more extreme than the Revisionist: others are actively opposed to the plan. But at the time of this writing (1945) it is not certain whether any of these committees will prove permanent or effective.

In 1929 the Zionist Organization and a group of Jewish leaders not affiliated with it undertook together to form the Jewish Agency for Palestine, which since that time has been recognized by the British Government as speaking for the Jews in all matters pertaining to the Holy Land.

IV

Another fissure in Judaism, which has arisen in modern times and which affects American Judaism to some extent though far less than it did that of central and eastern Europe, is the issue of language. The sacred language of the Jews throughout the ages has, of course, been Hebrew; and it seems probable that there never was a time when Hebrew did not continue to be a spoken language among some groups of Jews. While Aramaic in due time replaced it in Palestine and Babylonia, even as a language of discussion in schools and for the writing of rabbinic decisions, the kinship between the two Semitic tongues was such that Hebrew always remained a second language, at least, for the majority of scholars and educated Jews. Thus the basic books on Jewish law and life which were composed before the nineteenth century were almost all in Hebrew. The Jews of Arabic-speaking countries in the Middle Ages, however, used Arabic for important writings, such as the "Guide for the Perplexed" by Maimonides (which remains to this day the most important single contribution to the philosophy of Judaism). Because Arabic could easily be written in Hebrew characters, being like Aramaic a Semitic language, this adoption of the vernacular did not seem to constitute a real betrayal of the holy tongue; though no one ever suggested that prayers be offered in Arabic, or for that matter basic prayers in Aramaic. It is interesting to recall, however, that even so great a book as the "Guide" of Maimonides has served as a force in Judaism only in its Hebrew translation.

Jews who lived in lands where the vernacular was not

Semitic were naturally far more conscious of the difference between their ancient, sacred tongue and the common language of daily usage than were those of Aramaic and Arabic-speaking lands. Hence works on Judaism composed in Christian countries were all in Hebrew, or dialects based on the Talmudic mixture of Hebrew and Aramaic. Scholars corresponded with one another in Hebrew; all Jewish poetry, whether secular or religious, was for many centuries in Hebrew.

Because of widespread persecution and expulsions, in the fourteenth and fifteenth centuries there were large migrations of Jews from Germany into Poland and other parts of eastern Europe. In 1492 the Jews were finally expelled from Spain, and in 1496 from the remainder of the Iberian Peninsula. Both of these forced migrations had a curious effect on the Jews concerned. They retained in their new homes a deep affection for the culture and especially for the vernacular which they had brought with them. Consequently, Ladino, which is a development of Castilian, spoken by the Jewish emigrés from Spain in 1492, has been preserved until our own time as the language of their descendants; and Yiddish or Judaeo-German, which is a development of the language spoken by the fourteenth-century emigrés from Germany, remained the language of the Jews throughout central and eastern Europe.

The spread of west European nationalism to eastern Europe, the standardization of life throughout the world as a result of the Industrial Revolution, and the removal of the cultural and physical barriers which had narrowed Jewish life into a ghetto everywhere led during the course of the nineteenth century to three developments. Everywhere some Jews began to use the vernacular of their countries; others, reacting to the general enthusiasm for language as a group symbol, tried to resuscitate the use of Hebrew as a vernacular; and still others, in east European and central European countries, made a virtue of speaking and writing Yiddish. There thus arose among the Jews themselves a continuing struggle of language which has deeply affected Jewish thought.

In Lithuania, Poland, Russia, and other European countries, the rising labor groups among the Jews were especially vociferous in their devotion to Yiddish. It was, they maintained, the language of the people, whereas the vernacular of the country was that of the assimilated Jews, and Hebrew the language of the intellectuals. The struggle between these groups came to a head as a result of the provisions of the treaties established after World War I, which recognized the rights of linguistic minorities in certain countries to the maintenance of special schools. The division between the Yiddish-speaking and Hebrew-speaking groups became greater than ever, and their internecine struggles for the control of Jewish schools grew bitter.

In America, the struggle between the groups never became quite as sharp as in Europe, though each group made every effort to maintain its language as a language second to English for its children. There developed a number of Yiddish dailies and journals, Yiddish theaters, and Yiddish publishing houses. At present there are quite a few schools intended to instruct Jewish children after public school hours, in which the language of instruction is Yiddish and the main subjects are taken from Yiddish literature. On the other hand, there has been a strong movement to develop

Hebrew as a spoken language. This has succeeded to a degree; so that in a number of religious schools Hebrew is spoken quite freely, and a considerable, perhaps increasing, number of American Jews can read, write, and speak Hebrew.

The rise of Hebrew as a spoken and living language has been greatly stimulated by the fact that it has become the vernacular of the Palestinian Jewish community, and is officially recognized as one of the three legal languages of Palestine. There has thus resulted an astonishing revitalization of Hebrew literature, as well as Hebrew scholarship, both within and outside Palestine.

In America, Yiddish is still used as the language of preaching in many synagogues whose rabbis have been trained abroad, but English is rapidly displacing it. English is used as the main language of prayer in most Reform synagogues, though several ancient Hebrew portions are still kept. In Conservative and many Orthodox synagogues, the ancient Hebrew service is retained, but there are supplementary prayers in English, and the sermons are in English.

All of these divisions and interests probably are the concern of only a small number of Jewish men and women who are especially conscious of their heritage. The majority, or at least a large number, of Jews in the United States indicates no real interest in any of these issues. Many attend synagogue only on the Day of Atonement and New Year's Day; and the choice of a particular synagogue will depend less on conviction than on convenience. Most know little or no Hebrew, and recall Yiddish or Ladino only as the language of a revered grandparent. The Zionist issue is in the forefront of popular interest; nevertheless the official membership of the Zionist Organization of America is limited to a small minority, though it seems probable that a plebiscite would indicate widespread sympathy with Zionist aspirations among Jews who have any interest in Judaism.

There are, however, two aspects of Judaism which have developed large followings, and in which Jews are represented in large numbers. The first is the Jewish charitable foundations. For the vast majority of Jews in America philanthropy has become a mode of worship analogous to that of prayer and study in earlier generations. The participants even in the efforts of fund-raising seem to be satisfying a hunger for religious communion.

There have developed in the United States unprecedentedly strong Jewish organizations for philanthropy. In addition to the local organizations for charitable work, there is the United Jewish Appeal, which includes the American Jewish Joint Distribution Committee and the United Palestine Appeal. The sums raised by these organizations provide for sufferers abroad, and particularly for the needs of the Jewish settlement in Palestine. The various federations and welfare funds for fund-raising are now organized in a Council of Federations and Welfare Funds, which meets annually and helps local groups with their problems. The Hebrew Immigrant Aid Society does effective work in providing for the care of Jews on their arrival in the western hemisphere, particularly in the United States. The Ort Federation, organized during the period when European Jews included a disproportionate number of "intellectuals," for retraining them to serve as workers or as farmers, continues to serve in various communities both in Europe and the

Americas. There are numerous national and local women's and youth organizations which do outstanding work in various philanthropic and educational fields.

v

Another group of Jewish organizations with a large following are those established to protect the civil rights of Jews in various lands of persecution, and to bring about an understanding of Judaism by the general population. Judaism is not a missionary religion and seeks no converts. But the Jew has a duty to bring about an understanding of its principles by the world at large, so that the faith may win the respect even of those outside it.

This duty has become particularly important because of the urgent need to protect large Jewish communities against persecution and discrimination, due in large part to misunderstanding and ignorance. The rabbinic principle, "Who is the mightiest among the mighty? He who turns his enemy into a friend," applies to the Jewish people as a group, no less than to each individual. Hence leaders such as Louis Marshall, Felix M. Warburg, and Cyrus Adler considered it a religious obligation to organize efforts to counteract propaganda which was bringing Judaism and the Jews into disrepute and danger.

At present there are a number of American institutions which make an effort to deal with this type of evil. The oldest is the American Jewish Committee, founded in 1906 "to safeguard the civil and religious rights of Jews and to alleviate the consequences of persecution or disaster affecting them at home and abroad." The newer organizations, working in similar fields, are the Anti-Defamation League of the Independent Order B'nai B'rith, The American Jewish Congress, and the Jewish Labor Committee.

All four were for a time united in a General Jewish Council, but their special attitudes toward Judaism, their different social backgrounds, their varied ways of dealing with the intricate problem common to all, made coöperation difficult if not impossible. During the past few years there has been an effort to create an American Jewish Conference, which might deal with some of the problems of the Jews as a group, and in which all American Jews might be represented. But the American Jewish Conference has not succeeded in displacing its constituent organizations, and does not include a number of important Jewish groups.

The necessity of providing for the spiritual care and some of the social needs of Jews in the armed forces has led to the establishment of the Jewish Welfare Board. This organization is recognized by the War and Navy Departments as the Jewish agency for religious activities; it recommends chaplains to both services; provides articles for religious ceremonies for servicemen and women; publishes prayer books, etc. It is the Jewish constituent of the United Service Organizations. Recognized by all groups of Jews as their representative organization for these war functions, it also directs a number of peacetime communal activities, such as those of the local Y.M.H.A.'s and community centers.

The education of Jewish children is largely in the hands of the local congregations. But there are in many communities important institutions devoted wholly to Jewish education. These are usually called Talmud Torahs (study of the Torah). In these schools children receive instruction on

Sundays and on weekdays after regular school hours. There are in all communities Jewish day schools, modeled after the Catholic parochial schools, in which both religious and secular instruction is given. Such a school is often called a Yeshiva. The number of pupils attending these day schools has been rapidly increasing. In addition to the Talmud Torahs and Yeshivas which are primarily interested in the Jewish religion and in the Hebrew language, there are some which offer instruction in the history of the Jewish people as a group and in its culture, emphasizing the purely secular aspect of these phenomena and laying stress on the study of Yiddish. In general, these schools are maintained by the labor organizations.

Almost every considerable American Jewish community has an English-Jewish weekly, which helps its members keep in touch with the events of the Jewish world. There are also several syndicates providing materials for these weeklies: the best known are the Jewish Telegraphic Agency, the Independent Jewish Press Service, and the Seven Arts. The Jewish Telegraphic Agency also serves to keep the general press informed about matters of Jewish interest. Palcor is a competitor in this field.

In 1888 the Jewish Publication Society was organized to provide literature in English for the American Jewish reader. It has since published more than two hundred titles, including a number which have become classics, and distributed more than two and a half million volumes.

The many divisions among Jews and the multiplicity of their organizations may give the impression of incredible confusion. The days when Jews had an authoritative religious center to guide them are long past. The ancient Sanhedrin of Jerusalem is only a historical memory, as are the academies of Yabneh, of Tiberias, of Sura and Pumbedita in Babylonia. So, too, are the centers of authority which established themselves about the brilliant personalities of Rabbenu Gershom of Mayence in the tenth century; Rashi in the eleventh century; Maimonides in the twelfth century; and later teachers in subsequent generations. Even the authority of the Talmud is today being questioned by many, and rejected by a considerable number; so that there would seem to be no unifying factor in Judaism.

Curiously enough, there is a sense in which Jews are part of a single organic whole. The memories of a great tradition, the vague concept of a world service to be performed, the subtle influences of great teachers and works, even when not implicitly obeyed, are effective forces in guiding some of the conduct of all Jews, and much of the conduct of some Jews. In a world full of fragmentary information, confusion of motives, and self-contradictions, Judaism has its share of these deficiencies. But it is not formless, and it is not dying. The Jewish people is being compelled by social forces, too strong to resist, to follow the astonishingly profound insight which enabled the ancient Pharisaic schools of Shammai and Hillel to work together harmoniously, despite the vast differences of view between them. "The words of both groups," the Sages taught, "are the words of the living God." Something of this attitude toward difference is essential to the preservation and advancement of the Jewish heritage, as indeed of civilization generally in our complex world.

It is possible that the diversity of Judaism will not in our time give way to any monistic approach to the tradition; or even that the Jewish people will in the foreseeable future be organized so that any group of rabbis or scholars are recognized as authoritative by all. The Jewish people may remain for an indefinite period subject only to a consensus such as that in science, scholarship, letters, and art, in which, so far as any social compulsion is concerned, everyone is free to form his own judgment, and yet there are discernible vague, but definite, points of view, as the recognized doctrines of the group.

Such a unity, making possible coöperation without any element of social compulsion, requires a high development of the sense of individual responsibility to society, and dedication to the service of God. Indeed, it becomes daily more clear that Judaism can survive in the difficult age into which the world is moving, only if its people finally approach the ideal of the "kingdom of priests and the holy nation." Individuals are being driven by forces beyond their control to seek a moral and spiritual maturity which will make for teamwork despite independence of judgment; for collaboration despite wide difference of view and interest; for eagerness to share information, without seeking to impose ideas; for willingness to benefit by criticism both from within and from without the group. It may well be that the urgent need for reaching this standard of life and conduct, as a condition of survival, may yet lead to its realization in a degree which only a short time ago may have been considered improbable, if not impossible. If this development should occur, the sufferings which have made it possible and indispensable will prove a boon to mankind; for the example may lead to emulation on a far wider scale. There can be little doubt that before many generations the time must come when the differences among men will lead not to stratification and a caste system, but to the fructification and advancement of civilization; when the whole human species will rise to the level of a kingdom of priests and a holy nation. The "One World" which will emerge need not be a single empire or commonwealth or church or civilization, but an association of men entirely free and independent, and yet mutually loving; an association based on the close ties and informality of brotherhood, rather than on the bonds of formal organization; "an association to do the will of God with a perfect heart."

·5·

Humanism

THE end of the war will present two great questions—a question of government for the governors and a question of education for the teachers. There will be other questions as well. There will be bankers' questions for the bankers, and food questions for the farmers, and traders' questions for the traders, and military questions for the generals and the admirals. But the two great questions will be the questions of government and of education.

How do you govern in the new world with its invisible frontiers? And how do you educate the new people with their new possibilities of creation and destruction?

These two questions are serious. We can perhaps get along if the bankers fail to find an answer to the question of money—or refuse to accept the answer someone else finds for them. We can probably get along somehow whether or not the farmers find an answer to the question of food, and whether or not the traders learn how to trade, and the generals and admirals how to police the isthmuses and the oceans and the islands. But unless the governors—which means those who are governed as well—and the teachers—

which means also those who are taught—can find out how to govern the new world and how to educate men and women to live in it, we are quite literally lost. Lost not in rhetoric: lost in truth.

We used to say twenty-five years ago that the world couldn't survive another war. We thought we were making speeches. We know now that we were stating fact. The only parts of the world which will survive this war, except as ruins and fragments and remains, will be the parts of the world over which the war has not been fought. Next time, as the Nazis have obligingly shown us, there will be no margins. Planes which flew a few hundred miles with a few pounds of explosives in 1918 now fly thousands of miles with tons of explosives. Robot projectiles which now carry a ton of explosives a couple of hundred miles will increase both range and load in much the same way.

The lesson we have learned over the last few years is the lesson that "there are no neutrals in this war." In the next war—if there is a next war—the lesson we shall learn will be the lesson that there is no part of the world which is not a battlefield. Which means, not as a figure of speech but as a statement of fact, that what we understand by "the world" will not survive that war. Which means, in turn, that if there is another war our world is lost. Which means, finally, that we have no future worth thinking about unless we can learn, and learn quickly, to govern the world in such a way, and to educate its people in such a way, that another war will not occur.

When anyone talks about the crisis of humanism at the war's end, he is talking, if he is serious, about the answer humanism has to give, or ought to have to give, or ought to be allowed to have to give, to these two inescapable and desperate questions of government and education. He is not talking, that is to say, about the sad plight of the classics in the modern college, or the overemphasis on science in the current curriculum, or the lamentable discovery, in universities which had previously terminated all literature with the last rock on Land's End, that an American literature also exists. He is not talking, that is to say, in terms of academic politics or academic prestige or his own future as a professor. Above all, he is not talking about the effect of the Army training program on the academic economic system.

He is talking about the most urgent and most critical decisions to be taken in his time. And he is saying that a certain approach to these problems, a certain tradition of thought, a certain discipline, has something of importance to offer to their solution. He is saying that the tendency of the practical men among his contemporaries to exclude that approach and that discipline is dangerous. He is saying that it is dangerous, not to him and his academic fellows only, but to the practical men themselves—and to the world they share with us.

The serious question in all this discussion of the humanities, in other words, is the question whether the humanists and their discipline have, in fact, anything to offer to the solution of the two great moral and intellectual and political problems we must solve or perish. If they have not, if the humanists can claim no more than a decorative function in the preparation of young men for dinners-in-hall, then their disputes with their academic rivals, however brilliantly managed and however learnedly expressed, are hardly worth the present attention of living men. For one thing, living men have other and more urgent business to attend to. For another, they have every reason to remark that a philosophy of the education and life of man which has nothing to say to mankind about its life and education at the most critical moment in its recorded history is not a philosophy of man at all but a dilettantism with a pretentious name.

Both problems clearly fall within the field of humanist concern. Certainly the question of the role of education in the crisis of our time is a question on which the humanists can be expected to speak and by which they should expect to be judged. Humanism is at bottom a theory of the education proper to man and cannot therefore avoid judgment upon its position in the most solemn examination of educational theory the modern world has been obliged to undertake. On the contrary, humanism might well protest, and bitterly protest, its exclusion from that great assize.

The same thing is true, or so it seems to me, of the problem of government. Humanists, I realize, have not claimed the right in recent years to speak with authority of the art of government. Some of them may even decline that right today. Some of them, thinking of humanism as though it were a chapter in a university catalogue, may perhaps refuse to hold opinions on the art of government—on the ground that government is taught in the courses on political science and that the courses on political science are not usually given in the departments of humanities.

Others, taking a less curricular view, might conceivably renounce all right to be heard on the issue of government, and might decline to be judged by their contribution to its solution, on the ground that humanism is concerned with men solely as individuals and not with men in their relation to each other, or on the ground that humanism looks inward, not outward, or on the ground that humanism looks backward, not forward.

Philosophers of the ancient world would consider these to be strange limitations, I submit, upon the spiritual jurisdiction of a school which concerns itself with *humanitas*—with those things in man which are most manlike. Aulus Gellius defined *humanitas* by saying that earnest students of the liberal arts are most highly humanized because the knowledge they pursue is "granted to man alone of all the animals." Of the various forms of knowledge granted to man alone of all the animals, knowledge of the art of government is surely not the least.

Nor was it the least regarded in the past. It was not believed in Athens and Rome that the best education for man was an education unrelated to his practice of the art of government. On the contrary, it was assumed that a philosophy which thought in terms of the whole man, of the man in whom the manlike qualities were most developed, must necessarily have views not only on the training of those qualities but upon their exercise as well, and above all upon their noblest exercise—which would have included, in that time and in those cities, their exercise in government.

But there are other reasons than reasons of logic and history for the extension of humanistic jurisdiction, and therefore of humanistic responsibility, to the art of government. There are reasons of a practical nature. The humanistic renunciation of the public world has been happy neither for the public world nor for humanism. Humanism has become pallid with the pallor of all things grown within ivory walls; and government, once considered a noble art, has become at best a kind of profession and at worst a business. The recent uproar about Henry Wallace makes the point with an unintentional but appalling pertinence. Henry Wallace, said a characteristic article by one of the best-known of American journalists, is an exceptionally fine human being. He has a feeling for the tendency of things to come. But he is not at home and at ease in "the real world" and he is therefore, under the circumstances of the election, unacceptable for the Vice-presidency.

Whatever may be said of opinion about Henry Wallace, the view of statesmanship there expressed is one a humanist might challenge and, in my opinion, should. Indeed both humanism and statesmanship would be healthier today if the humanists had challenged the businessman's view of the art of government before it produced the generations of leaders "at home in the real world" who conducted Western civilization through so much of the nineteenth century and the twentieth to the situation in which we find ouselves today. It would be difficult to prove that there would have been more Lincolns and Jeffersons if the humanists had not forsaken the public world, but it must be obvious that there would almost certainly have been fewer Coolidges and Tafts.

II

I propose to assume, therefore, and for the purposes of this discussion, that humanism can be expected to supply an answer to the two critical questions of how to govern and how to teach. It remains therefore to consider whether the answer humanism can be expected to offer is or is not entitled to a better hearing than it has had.

But that consideration turns, of course, upon the nature of the humanist answer. There are almost as many definitions of humanism and the humanities as there are men who have written them. If one assumes, for example, that the humanities are what Webster calls "the branches of polite learning," especially belles-lettres and the ancient classics, and that humanism is merely a scholarly devotion to these studies, there will be some difficulty in persuading a tortured world that humanism and the humanities have much to say to it.

Polite learning, it will be objected, is all very well for a polite age, and knowledge of the ancient classics and of beautiful letters is a charming embellishment in a serene and spacious time; but for us, bewildered and frightened in a chaotic and savage world in which all the landmarks are lost and all the assurances washed away, the book beneath the classic bough is a mockery and a delusion. We have First Things to learn again before we can learn Last Things. We must learn again how to survive—how to keep the peace; how to restrain the wild beasts and the violence. Keep your culture, the world might well say, until we can build a quiet room to house it in—until we can be certain that the house of culture will stand at least for a generation at a time; until the skies are quiet again and a place for stars, not for the most terrible and insensate death and the swiftest destruction.

And there will be much the same objection if you define your humanist as the perfect type of intellectual aristocrat, living a life of reflection and criticism above the battle and the common dust. You will be told that such a man, if he does not make himself a prig in the process, may well become an ornament in a world which has room for ornaments, but that we, who must buttress and rebuild our lives before chaos engulfs them, have no time to think of such luxuries as a natural aristocracy of learning and of taste.

So again if you adopt the definition of humanism which describes it as a form of intellectual discipline—the discipline of the intellect for its own sake rather than for the sake of proficiency in some art, or craft, or profession. Rude persons will tell you that to cultivate the mind for its own sake one must first have leisure, and that to have leisure one must be able to foretell the time, and that in our world a man cannot foretell the time since the time is already past and nothing is sure and each day is more dangerous than the last and a man can only prepare himself for disaster or survival.

It will be the same, too, even if you take the more generous definition in which humanism appears as that method of education and that practice of life of which the purpose is to free the faculties of men for their fullest exercise and their finest development. To free the faculties of men for their fullest exercise is a noble purpose. But its end, as someone will be unkind enough to point out, is not a free man, —a man committed to freedom as well as possessed of it,— but rather a *freed* man—a man freed of all commitments, including the commitment to freedom itself.

Such an end, however enchanting it may seem in a peaceful time when men can afford the after-dinner sport of questioning everything and giving themselves to nothing, has an irresponsible and even a frivolous look to a generation which has been compelled to think of freedom as something you were either prepared to die for or prepared to lose. To be free of every prejudice, including the prejudice of freedom, may make a man superior, but it can hardly endear him, for the moment at least, to those who have offered their lives precisely to defend the prejudice that freedom has a supreme and absolute worth. Moral eclecticism looks curiously out of place among the dead wreaths and the fading cotton flags of the soldiers' cemeteries. It is particularly out of place when the certainty of the soldier's grave that freedom was worth dying for is the only certainty men have to hold to. To offer to teach the men of such a generation how to avoid the pitfalls of prejudice and excessive belief is indeed to offer stones to those who starve for bread.

III

The fact is that the humanism of these various definitions is a humanism which finds its reason in the fifteenth century rather than our own—in the fifteenth century and in those later centuries in which, as in the fifteenth, the sickness of the soul was dogma and superstition. Humanism considered as an intellectual discipline-for-discipline's-sake, or as a regimen to free the mind of prejudice and infatuation, or as an aristocratic training of the taste, or as a cult of the classic past, or as the appreciation of fine arts and beautiful letters, is a prime specific for such ills as bigotry and puritanism and jesuitry and vulgarity and Victorianism and the complacency of the bourgeois mind. But humanism so conceived has little if anything to say to a time in which the spiritual sickness is not excess of belief but lack of belief. And ours, if we understand the ills we suffer from, is such a time.

We have valued liberty enough to fight for it, and we know very well what enemy we detest, but the affirmative cause, not only of the war but of our lives, escapes us. When we debate, as we have debated endlessly, the question of what we are fighting for, we have sometimes thought it was what we are living for we needed most to know. The weakness is not in the time, we think, but in ourselves. We have seen whole peoples deliver their lives and purposes and wills to tyrants they themselves have invented out of a loud voice and a blathering mouth and a ridiculous uniform to satisfy the hunger of their fear. We have seen others who cried out for a great conversion of the world, a vast revival, a wind from beyond the planet and the stars, to fill us in spite of ourselves, and without our effort, by some miracle of faith, like the miracle they imagine to have happened when Christianity first took the world, or when the religion of the Prophet took it.

Everywhere in our time there are the signs and indications of a passion to believe, a passion to escape from the sense of human inadequacy which spreads and deepens as science and the mechanical arts disclose the enormous scale and the terrible potentialities of a universe vaster and more dangerous than men, before our generation, had imagined. The natural sciences open fissures in the skin of the earth and the cover of the sky which lead beyond human meaning. The specialists press their narrow drills of research outward and away from the human center of experience. The libraries overflow with a flood of printed pages, and knowledge has become too vast for men to know.

The world, we say to ourselves, is too large for us, too difficult to understand, too savage to restrain, too swift to master. It is no longer a world to be measured in distance by a man's foot, or in time by a man's sleeping and waking, or in danger by a man's strength or an animal's. It is a world beyond the capacity of men to control—a world that needs gods or men like gods. And so we long for the men like gods, or for the gods, to believe in.

Humanists may regret this hunger to believe, but they will be foolish, notwithstanding, if they ignore the longing of their generation; and worse than foolish if they do not see the significance of that longing to themselves and to their cause. For the meaning of our longing for belief is this: that we have lost our sense of the place of man in the universe.

It is to a generation which has lost this sense that the humanists now must offer what they have to teach. If they do not understand the significance of that fact to the philosophy they protest; if they persist in declaring that what they have to teach is a method only, a gymnastic, or at the best an antidote, a cleansing salt, an antiseptic; if they are unwilling to turn their questions into answers for a time that needs their answers—then they have themselves to thank, and not the blunders of the Army and the Navy, or the blindness of their colleagues in the universities, for the indifference of which they now complain.

IV

For there is a definition of humanism by which human-ism becomes a belief in the one thing in which man has greatest need now to believe—himself, and the dignity and importance of the place he fills in the world he lives in. There is a definition of humanism by which humanism be-comes precisely the belief of man in his own dignity, in his essential worth as a man, in what Ralph Barton Perry calls "his characteristic perfection": a belief not in the potenti-ality of man, but in the actuality of man; a belief not in the classic perfection of the beautiful letters men have written in the distant past, but in the human perfection of the men who wrote those letters and of others like them, whether writers or others than writers, and whether living in the past or in the present or not yet born; a belief not in the thing a man may become if he reads the right books and develops the right tastes and undergoes the right discipline, but a belief in the thing he is.

No one has put this better than Professor Perry in his superb *Definition of the Humanities.* "The reference to man in the context of the so-called 'humanities,'" he says, "is . . . not descriptive or apologetic, but eulogistic; not 'human—all too human,' or 'only human,' but human in the sense in which one deems it highest praise to be called 'a man.'" The answer humanism has it in its power to make to the two great questions, how to govern and how to teach, is the answer of belief in man, "in the sense in which one deems it highest praise to be called 'a man.'" If the world can be taught to believe in the worth of man, in the dignity of man, in the "characteristic perfection" of man, it can be taught not only to survive but to live. If the world can be governed in belief in the worth of man, in the dignity of man, it can be governed in peace.

These propositions need no proof. They speak for themselves. If government throughout the world were directed by a convinced belief in the dignity of man as man, in the worth of man as man, so that decisions of government were everywhere made in consonance with that belief and in furtherance of it, no one can doubt that the world would be well governed and that peace would be as nearly certain as peace can be in a variable universe. It is lack of faith in the essential dignity and worth of man which corrupts and weakens democratic governments, substituting for a government by the people in the people's interest, which is peace, a government of rulers in the rulers' interest—which may be war. It is doubt of the dignity and worth of man which opens the road to the tyrannies and dictatorships which have no choice but war. It is cynical contempt for the worth and dignity of man which makes the wars of the dictators wars of slavery and subjugation.

If the fundamental proposition upon which the government of the world was based were the proposition that man, because he is man, and in his essential quality as man, has worth and value which governments exist to serve and to protect, regardless of race and regardless of color or religion, there would be little room for the play of international politics which, under color of realism or under color of necessity, puts power first or oil first or gold first, and men second or nowhere, preparing thus for the wars of power or of oil or gold. If the first business of government everywhere were man, the whole man of the humanists; if the first object of government everywhere were the good of man, man "in the sense in which one deems it highest praise to be called 'a man' "; if the first principle of government everywhere were the principle that government exists for man and not man for government, there would be no place for the governments of which the first business is business, or for the governments of which the first object is economic advantage, or for the governments of which the first principle is power.

But to govern in this way it is necessary first of all to believe, and not merely to declare that one believes, in the fundamental worth and value of man and to practice that belief and never to cease to practice it. It is necessary to believe in man, not only as the Christians believe in man, out of pity, or as the democrats believe in man, out of loyalty, but also as the Greeks believed in man, out of pride.

v

The same thing is true of the question how to teach. If education were informed with a belief in the dignity and worth of man; if the purpose of education were an understanding not only of the weaknesses of man and the sicknesses of man and the failures of man but of the essential nobility of man also, of his "characteristic perfection," men would be able again to occupy their lives and to live in the world as the Greeks lived in it, free of the bewilderment and frustration which has sent this generation, like the Gadarene swine, squealing and stumbling and drunk with the longing for immolation, to hurl themselves into the abysses of the sea.

If science were taught, not as something external to man,

something belittling of man, but as one of the greatest of the creations of the human spirit; if economics were taught not as a structure of deterministic laws superior to man and controlling his conduct, but as one of the many mirrors man has constructed to observe the things he does; if history and descriptive literature were taught not as peepholes through which the unworthy truth about mankind may be observed but as expressions of man's unique ability and willingness to see and judge himself; if belief in man and in his dignity and worth became the controlling principle of education, so that the people of the world were taught to respect the common principle of humanity in others and in themselves, and to believe that their lives would be shaped and their future determined not by some law of economics, or by some formula of science, or by some regimen of the subconscious, but by their own wills and on their own responsibility—if these things could be accomplished, who will doubt that the sense of irresponsibility and frustration which has driven so many millions of our contemporaries down the blind steep of slavery into war could be corrected?

The task education must accomplish, if free societies are to continue to exist, is the re-creation of the sense of individual responsibility—which means the reëstablishment of the belief of men in man. Fascism is only another name for the sickness and desperation which overcome a society when it loses its sense of responsibility for its own life and surrenders its will to a tyrant it, and it alone, has invented. But the sense of responsibility in a nation is a sense of responsibility in the individuals who compose that nation, for the sense of responsibility is always a charge upon the individual conscience and vanishes when many share it. And to re-create the sense of individual responsibility it is necessary to restore the belief of men in man—the belief that man can direct his destiny if he will.

It is impossible to charge the consciences of men with responsibility for the world they live in without convincing them that they can act upon their world—that the power to decide and act is theirs. No one knew that better than Abraham Lincoln, who knew many things about the human soul. When it became necessary for him, in the terrible December of 1862, to drive home to the Congress a sense of its responsibility, he used these words:

Fellow citizens, we cannot escape history. We of this Congress and this Administration will be remembered in spite of ourselves. No personal significance or insignificance can spare one or another of us. The fiery trial through which we pass will light us down, in honor or dishonor, to the latest generation. . . . We—even we here—hold the power and bear the responsibility.

What education in the free countries must drive home, if the free countries are to survive, is the conviction that we—even we here—hold the power and bear the responsibility. The task is in part a task beyond the power of the schools as such, for the sense of individual responsibility and power involves a sense of individual participation, and a sense of individual participation is only possible in a society in which individuals can make themselves felt directly and not through agglomerations of money or people. There must be social changes as well as educational changes. But the educational changes come first. Not until men believe that the responsibility can be theirs to bear, and therefore should be theirs to bear, will they make it theirs. To teach men to believe in themselves therefore is to teach them responsibility and so to assure their freedom.

VI

These, as I understand humanism, are the answers the humanists have it in their power to give to their time and to the questions their time has asked of them. They are answers which seem to me to be true and to dispose, once and for all, of the question whether humanism has anything to say to the generation to which we belong. Any school, any philosophy, which can go as close to the root of the essential sickness of our time has a right to be heard, and may claim that right, and may denounce fairly and justly those who deprive it of that right, pretending that other points of view are more practical and therefore more important.

But these answers are not the answers, as I read the record, which the humanists—all the humanists at least— are willing to give. On the contrary, many humanists would reject them, and reject them for a reason which goes very deep. They would reject them because the dignity of man in which they believe is not the dignity implicit in these answers—is not, that is to say, a dignity which men possess because they are men, but only a dignity which men may earn by undergoing certain disciplines and acquiring certain characteristics.

Man, to these humanists, is not born with worth, but may acquire worth. Until he has earned it he has no right or reason to believe in himself, nor should a belief in man determine the attitude in which he is to be ruled. Humanism to these humanists, in other words, is not a democratic doctrine on which a practice of self-government can be founded, but an aristocratic doctrine which, because its concern is inward, has little to say of government of any kind. It is, if anything, a doctrine opposed to democracy and to theories of the universal worth of man, because excellence, not equality, is its goal and purpose.

It would be a mistake to dismiss these humanists as dwellers in towers, or their definitions as definitions of refuge. The passion for excellence can be a sword as well as a sanctuary. Committed to the love of the arts and the great books and the monuments of unaging intellect, as Yeats so wonderfully called them, and the courtesies and graces and perceptions of a civilized and generous life, the worshipers of excellence have waged war, and noble war, against an increasing vulgarity which has won its greatest triumphs in our time, having found the mechanical means at last to intrude its coarseness into every hour, however private, and every chamber, however secret, of our lives.

Those to whom humanism is the worship of excellence do not admit, as they look around them in the streets and trains and hotel lobbies of our world, that all men have dignity and worth. They do not believe, as they look back across the centuries to the world they imagine to have existed in Athens and in Rome, that all men are able to govern themselves or should be allowed to. They do not agree, as they face the crisis of our time, that freedom is the answer to everything. They do not necessarily hold with public freedom. The freedom they seek is inward in the large and lofty world of enlightened intellect where learning paints the various landscape and a trained and delicate taste selects the road. That there must be peace and quiet outside the mind, if a man is to journey within it, they readily admit. But the peace without, they say, is not their business.

VII

It is understandable enough that men should love what these men love, and hate what they hate. Their ideal of the truly civilized man is in every way admirable. Their contempt for a world in which taste is determined in advertising agencies, and intelligence is measured by the answers children give to questions on the air, is a contempt which later generations of Americans will not find strange. But what is not understandable is their choice of the word humanism to describe their inward and selective life. Humanism as a word cannot cut itself off from its root or forget its derivation. Humanism, to deserve the *humanitas* from which it comes, must incorporate some notion of things appropriate to every man as man—things worthy of man in every man.

It must incorporate, that is to say, some notion of a universal dignity which men possess as men and by virtue of their manhood. The dignity of man upon which a philosophy of man, a school devoted to man, is based cannot be a rare and sought-for attribute which only the school can teach man to acquire and only the philosophy aid man to deserve. You do not construct out of the airy goal at which you hope to arrive the solid ground from which you depart. You do not derive the dignity of man on which your philosophy is founded from the dignity which those few who practice your philosophy can claim to possess. The dignity of man is either here and now or it is never. It is either in mankind or it is nowhere.

One can no more make an aristocracy of human dignity than one can make an aristocracy of human love or human curiosity, or any other fundamental human characteristic. Some men will develop their manlike qualities farther than others. Some will be more learned, have surer taste, livelier imagination, greater gentility—will be, in brief, more civilized than others. But whatever the degree of their development, the qualities with which the true humanist is concerned are the manlike qualities—the qualities which men possess because they are men; the qualities, therefore, which all men possess to one degree or another. It is man whom the humanist values, and man is in all men—*is* all men.

To limit humanism, therefore,—to put a narrower construction upon it than this,—is quite literally to deprive it of its fundamental meaning. It is as though a select association of superior and cultivated people were to call themselves the association of mankind. The word mankind, in such a context, would have an ironic meaning or have none at all. So humanism, if its concern is not man, and therefore all men, has only an ironic meaning or has none. But founded on the universal human basis which its root implies, the name becomes a noble and intelligible word with meanings which our time needs more than any others.

This war is a war against those who, in contempt of man and in despair of man's power to direct his life, have surrendered their lives into the hands of tyrants they themselves have created. It is a war against the philosophy of contempt for man and despair of his future which those who have surrendered their lives have invented to justify themselves, or have accepted from their masters. It is a war therefore in which the issue is, in last analysis, the issue of man—of the concept of man which is to shape and control our time; of the idea of man which governments are to reflect and societies to mirror.

We, on our side, have found it easy to put our cause into negative words, into words of resistance. We are opposed to the philosophy of contempt for man and to those who accept that philosophy: we have seen what it does to those who practice it and to those upon whom it is practiced also. But we have not found it easy to put our cause into the affirmative words of our own purpose. And for this reason: that the affirmative statement of our cause is a declaration of belief in man, and we have not been altogether ready and willing to make that declaration, since we too have felt the winds of fear and doubt which turned our enemies to disbelievers. More than anything else, we need a rebirth of belief in ourselves as men. If humanism will make itself the instrument of that renaissance of man, its place, not only in the universities but in the world, is sure. For if it will make itself that instrument it will give our time its cause.

NOTE: An address delivered in Madison, Wisconsin, this paper was published under the title "Humanism and the Belief in Man" in the *Atlantic Monthly* for November, 1944, from which it is here reprinted by permission.